W9-CCR-184

To All ETERNITY

Presented to

George Wilderman

By

On

September Twelve, 2009

Gaudenzio Ferrari (1475–1546). *Musical Angels.*
(Detail.)

To All ETERNITY

The Essential Teachings of Christianity

Written by

Edward Engelbrecht, Edward Grube, Raymond Hartwig, Jeffrey Kunze,
Erik Rottmann, Rodney Rathmann, Harold Senkbeil

Calligraphy by

Edward Q. Luhmann

CONCORDIA PUBLISHING HOUSE · SAINT LOUIS

Second edition
Copyright © 2002, 2004 Concordia Publishing House
3558 S. Jefferson Avenue
St. Louis, MO 63118-3968

All rights reserved. Unless specifically noted, no part of this publication may be reproduced, stored in a retrieval system,
or transmitted, in any form or by any means, electronic, mechanical, photocopying, recording, or otherwise,
without the prior written permission of Concordia Publishing House.

Project managed by Joseph Snyder

Edited by Edward Engelbrecht

Designed by Jacqueline Appelt and Edward Q. Luhmann

Editor's translation of Romans 13:13–14

All other Scripture quotations are from the HOLY BIBLE, NEW INTERNATIONAL VERSION®. NIV®.
Copyright © 1973, 1978, 1984 by International Bible Society.
Used by permission of Zondervan Publishing House. All rights reserved.

This publication may be available in braille, in large print, or on cassette tape for the visually impaired.
Please allow 8 to 12 weeks for delivery.
Write to the Library for the Blind, 7550 Watson Rd., St. Louis, MO 63119-4409;
call toll-free 1-888-215-2455; or visit the Web site: www.blindmission.org.

Manufactured in Spain

1   2   3   4   5   6   7   8   9   10   13   12   11   10   09   08   07   06   05   04

To Lauritz and Doris Jensen
and all faithful students and teachers
of God's holy Word

Contents

Contents

Ways to Use To All Eternity

Conversation Starter. Proudly display your copy of *To All Eternity* on your coffee table. Browse while you watch TV or rest. Invite visitors to view and discuss your favorite paintings and passages.

Lenten Devotional. Beginning on Ash Wednesday, read one devotion each day throughout the season of Lent (you will finish the book during the first week of Easter). Start each meditation by reciting aloud the particular commandment, passage of the creed, or the like. Thoughtfully view the painting and read the accompanying devotional page. Ask yourself the following devotional questions:

Change: How does this teaching point out the need for change in my life?

Blessing: What promises and blessings does the Lord give me in this teaching?

Praise: In view of this teaching, what praise will I express to the Lord?

Request: What requests will I make of the Lord?

Close your meditation with your personal prayers. To enhance your reflections, write your thoughts and prayers in a journal or diary.

One-Year Devotional. Begin any time of year by meditating on each painting and devotion for one week in the following ways.

Monday: Read the devotional article and ask yourself the Change, Blessing, Praise, and Request questions listed above.

Close your meditation with your personal prayers.

Tuesday through Saturday: Recite aloud the particular commandment, passage of the creed, or the like. Read the Bible passage and meditation question for the day. Note: These are *meditation* questions. Read—even reread—the Bible passage and seek your answer in the text (Psalm 1:2). Continue with the Change, Blessing, Praise, and Request questions listed above.

Ask God to give you a deeper understanding of your life in view of His teaching. To enhance your meditation, write your thoughts and prayers in a journal or diary. Close your meditation with your personal prayers.

Sunday: Attend public worship.

Small-group Use of *To All Eternity.* Consider sharing your devotional time with a family member or friend. Gather weekly with fellow users of the book to discuss what you have learned. Share your insights and prayer requests. Offer praise to the Lord by singing hymns.

Preface

A, B, C . . . recites the poet as she turns each page,
searching for just the right word.

1, 2, 3 . . . counts the architect as he reviews the blueprints,
building a new city block.

Some lessons we never outgrow. The alphabet we recite and the numbers we count—we need them day by day.

In a similar way, Christians never outgrow their first lessons in the faith. Truths such as the Ten Commandments, the Apostles' Creed, and the Lord's Prayer remain part of daily living and believing. Like letters and numbers, they form our thoughts and guide our lives. We will use them . . . to all eternity.

Through dramatic visuals and stirring meditations, the following pages will acquaint you with the essential teachings of Christianity. Whether you are a new Christian seeking deeper understanding or a mature Christian seeking renewed strength, this book will enlighten and inspire you. It draws its outline from one of the most popular books of Christian devotion next to the Bible itself: the Small Catechism of Dr. Martin Luther. For almost 500 years, Christians of all denominations have hailed Luther's "little book" for its profound simplicity. As you read, consider the countless people who have scanned these words before you and used them to form their prayers.

I believe in God . . .

> *confesses a child, expressing his fledgling faith.*

Our Father who art in heaven . . .

> *prays a grandmother, abiding in God's grace . . .*
> *to all eternity.*

Marie Spartali Stillman (1844–1927). *Beatrice.*

So Many Religions . . .

In 1804 the emperor Napoleon declared freedom of religion for all subjects in his territories. Many people hailed this decree as an answer to centuries of debate about religion and government. However, people soon realized that debate was far from over. Although the freedom to practice one's religion greatly encouraged millions of people, such freedom provided no answer to a more basic problem: throughout the world there are many religions, each with different teachings and practices. As a result, many people are confused. They wonder, "How can I know which religion is true, which one will truly guide me with God's wisdom and not just the opinions of men?"

Which One Is Right?

All religions of the world have at least one thing in common: they all tell you how you should live. They distinguish between right and wrong. In other words, all religions proclaim the Law.

The Law is an important teaching and answers many practical questions, such as "How should I take care of my family and treat my neighbor?" But the Law also presents a devastating problem: all of us fail to keep the Law as we should. We do not live up to God's standards of right and wrong. Because even religious people cannot keep the Law, they may live in constant doubt of God's love for them. Instead of offering joy, peace, and comfort, Law-based faith becomes a terror to those who live by it.

However, one religion differs from all the others because it not only proclaims the Law but also—more importantly—the Gospel, the promise of salvation and forgiveness for all who break God's Law. While most religions can teach you about right and wrong behavior, only Christianity offers the Gospel of salvation, which releases you from all doubt and fear. Through the Gospel teachings of Jesus Christ, you will receive more than just rules. As the Bible says, you will receive "the peace of God, which transcends all understanding" (Philippians 4:7). If you crave a deeper understanding of God, His love, and eternal peace, then be sure to read and carefully study this book based on the teachings of the Bible. It will help you understand . . .

the one religion that offers peace with God through the Gospel!

Prologue

Fra Angelico (1387–1455). The Conversion of St. Augustine. (Detail.)

Meditations: Change Blessing Praise Request

^MRead the article on page 13. ^{Tu}Romans 6:1–6. How does Baptism change the heart?
^WJohn 15:1–8. Why does the Lord "prune" as well as "nurture"?
ThPsalm 119:9–16. What aid has God given you to guide and bless your life?
^FLuke 15:11–24. How does God receive the broken-hearted?
^SPhilippians 4:4–9. Describe the peace that God gives.

A young man sat quietly in a peaceful garden outside his friend's home in Milan, Italy. Although nature's beauty and serenity surrounded him, inwardly his heart churned with turmoil. For years the young man had devoted himself to various philosophies and religions as he searched for a joyful and peaceful life. He had tried the teachings of the famous Greek philosopher Plato. He had joined a radical religious group. He had thoroughly studied classic works of literature. But despite all of this, his heart remained restless.

Perhaps, like this young man, you have sought peace and meaning for your life, only to end up discouraged and restless of heart. Don't give up hope! Through Baptism and faith in Christ, your heavenly Father will drive away all your doubts. Through the Gospel of His Son, Jesus Christ, God will grant you peace that lasts to all eternity.[Tu]

Peace with God

As a child, the man pictured here had heard about Christianity from his mother and had read some portions of the Bible. But he had never been baptized into the Christian faith. Now, at the age of 32, realizing that his life was out of control, he sat in the beautiful garden, stared at his feet, and wondered what would become of him.[W]

As he sat quietly, he noticed a book beside him, left outside by his friend. It contained part of the Bible—the letters of St. Paul. The young man picked it up, turned the pages, and began to read. His eyes fell upon these words: "[Live] not in riots and drunken parties, not in eroticism and indecencies, not in strife and rivalry, but put on the Lord Jesus Christ" (Romans 13:13–14).[Th]

Peace through Christ

Through these simple words, God set to work on the young man's troubled heart. Through the Law, God showed the young man what was wrong with his life, how he lived for himself—his own pleasure and success—instead of living for God.[F] Then the heavenly Father pointed the young man toward Jesus, whose message of forgiveness and new life penetrated the young man's heart and changed his life. He became a sincere follower of Jesus. We know him today as St. Augustine.

As you study God's Word of Law and Gospel, God will work in your heart just as He worked in the heart of St. Augustine. Through His Law, God will show you your sin. But through the Gospel of Jesus Christ, your heavenly Father will forgive you and transform you. He will calm your restless heart and give you peace that lasts to all eternity.[S]

Respect
Obey
Honor
Word
Love

the Ten

THE FIRST

THE SECOND *

THE THIRD

THE FOURTH

THE FIFTH

THE SIXTH

THE SEVENTH

THE EIGHTH

THE NINTH

THE TENTH

COMMANDMENTS

Ex 20:3-4,5,6

You shall have no other gods. 56 - 61

You shall not misuse the name of the Lord your God. 61 - 67   Ex 20:7

Remember the Sabbath day by keeping it holy. 67 - 73   Ex 20:8-11

Honor your father and your mother. 74 - 76   Ex 20:12

You shall not murder. 77 - 80   Ex 20:13   Ex. 20

You shall not commit adultery. 81 - 85   Ex 20:14

You shall not steal. 85 - 87   Ex 20:15

You shall not give false testimony against your neighbor. 87 - 89   Ex 20:16

You shall not covet your neighbor's house. Ex 20:17   89 - 90

You shall not covet your neighbor's wife, or his manservant or maidservant,
his ox or donkey, or anything that belongs to your neighbor. Ex 20:17   91 - 92

*The Bible does not specifically number each commandment. As a result, different numbering traditions have arisen.
 For example, some denote Exodus 20:4 as the Second Commandment.

15

Karl Pavlovitch Briullov (1799–1852). *The Last Days of Pompeii.*

You shall have no other gods.

What does this mean? We should fear, love, and trust in God above all things.

Meditations: Change Blessing Praise Request

M Read the article on page 17. Tu Exodus 32:9–16. How did God's promise save Israel here?
W Isaiah 44:16–23. Reflect on what man makes and what God makes. Th 1 Corinthians 8:1–6. How do we "live"? Why?
F Hebrews 12:18–29. What will God do (verses 26–27)? S Psalm 18:7–19. Contrast the actions of God's hands.

Marble, a substance usually considered permanent, totters and pops as Mount Vesuvius shakes the earth. The wealthy Romans of Pompeii hold one another as their polished marble idols fall. The ashen remains of Pompeii show how fragile life is. Ruined gods and goddesses teach the foolishness of holding on to what will not last.

In the First Commandment, your heavenly Father makes your need clear. As the challenges of life shake you each day, you need something sure to cling to—something that cannot be shaken. As illustrated here, the issue is not what you hold but *who* holds you.[Tu]

An Ever-Changing World

What you hold in your hands, your possessions and securities, cannot prop you up or comfort you. At best, like the polished marble idols of Pompeii, they will distract you from your only true help: the Lord.

The First Commandment compels us to see the works of our hands for what they really are—unstable idols in an ever-changing world.[W] Having "no other gods" means more than simply believing that there is only one God. It means fearing and respecting God's authority, loving God above everything else, and trusting in God alone for your life and salvation.

God created you. God sustains heaven and earth despite the ravages of sin and rebellion.[Th] In your moment of need, He will not shake. To rescue you from worthless idols, He sent His own dear Son, Jesus Christ, to hold your life together.

He Holds You

The Bible tells us that when Jesus carried the cross through the streets of Jerusalem, He tottered beneath its awful weight. He dropped to the dust, a broken man. He bore these pains so that He might prepare a permanent home for you—a kingdom that cannot be shaken.[F] On Easter Sunday, Jesus shook the earth. The stone covering Jesus' tomb rolled back, and He stepped forth again into the lives of His disciples.

After the eruption of Vesuvius, no one trusted the ash-covered idols of Pompeii. After the resurrection, millions continue to trust in Jesus Christ. Don't let anything or anyone come between you and your Lord. He holds you this day as His most precious child. Though all else falls away, His hands remain firm. He will hold on to you.[S]

The nurse called out for me to look at the clock down the hall and tell her the time. I told her I couldn't see the time. She popped out of the patient's room, turned toward the clock, and said, "You can't see that?" She pulled off her glasses. "You must be nearsighted. Tell me if this helps."

I slipped her glasses on. Suddenly, I saw everything clearly. I had forgotten just how much detail the world has. Poor vision, even blindness, can really sneak up on you. After years in a blur, I finally saw how much I was missing. I immediately called an eye doctor for help.

Losing Sight

Just as physical blindness can sneak up on you, so can spiritual blindness. For example, during college I stopped going to church. Without realizing the full effects of what I was doing, I hid my eyes from God's Word and neglected to call on His name.[Tu]

My spiritual sight was near blindness. Though I believed that Jesus was my Savior, I lived in a fog. Though I still prayed, I never really called out for the help my soul needed. Thankfully, the Lord always saw my need clearly.

Call on the Lord's Name

Poussin's painting *Christ Healing the Blind at Jericho* illustrates the Lord's compassion not only for these blind men but also for you and me.[W] The blind men in the picture had heard from others that help was nearby. They heard that Jesus could heal their blindness.

Seeing their opportunity, they called on His name: "Lord, Son of David, have mercy on us!" With love and patience, Jesus stopped to hear their cry. He touched their eyes and opened them. In faith, the men followed Him.

The Lord showed similar compassion to me. He placed certain friends in my life who gently encouraged me to call on the Lord's name. Back to the Word! To see clearly what the Lord has to say. Back into worship! To follow the Lord, refreshed and renewed. Back home! With renewed vision, I realized how much I had missed. In fact, I felt foolish for letting myself stray as far as I did.[Th] Yet I thanked the Lord for hearing my cry. I praised Him for reaching out to me and healing my spiritual shortsightedness.[F]

New Focus

The Lord will bring your life into sharper focus. He will touch you with His love and heal your blindness. He will open your eyes so that you might see the seriousness of your sins. But He will also bring you the cross, where He paid for every one of those sins in full.[S]

Nicolas Poussin (1594–1665). *Christ Healing the Blind at Jericho.*

You shall not misuse the name of the Lord your God.

What does this mean? We should fear and love God so that we do not curse, swear, use satanic arts, lie, or deceive by His name, but call upon it in every trouble, pray, praise, and give thanks.

Meditations: Change Blessing Praise Request
M Read the article on page 18. Tu 2 Corinthians 4:1–6. What causes spiritual blindness?
W Psalm 116. What reason do you have to call upon God's name?
Th Matthew 20:29–34. What can you learn from these blind men? F 1 Chronicles 16:7–18. Glory in God's name.
S Isaiah 29:18–24. What will the eyes of God's people see?

Pieter Brueghel the Elder (1525/30–1569). *Fight between Carnival and Lent.* (Detail.)

Remember the Sabbath day by keeping it holy.

What does this mean? We should fear and love God so that we do not despise preaching and His Word, but hold it sacred and gladly hear and learn it.

Meditations: Change Blessing Praise Request
MRead the article on page 21.
TuMark 2:23–3:5. What is the purpose of the Sabbath? WIsaiah 55:6–11. What does God's Word do?
ThColossians 1:15–23. How does Christ present you to God? FRevelation 19:1–10. Reflect on the benefits of the Lord's Supper.
SHebrews 10:19–25. Encourage others to worship.

Some Christians think worship means rules: "Fast during Lent! Worship the way we tell you! Do this! Do that!" Others respond with the opposite extreme: "Party!" they cry. "Worship however you please!" Still others reject worship entirely, saying, "I don't need to go to church to be Christian."

This painting ridicules the age-old worship struggle by portraying it as a jousting match. Pulled by a monk and a nun, Lady Lent represents all who require man-made worship laws.[Tu] She attacks Prince Carnival, whose followers abuse their Gospel freedom by doing whatever they please.

Making Worship Their Own Work

Even though these groups oppose each other, they make the same mistake. Both groups fail to realize the power of God's life-giving Word.[W]

Lady Lent's group thinks of worship as a human activity that responds to God's command. This group hopes that its many rules and regulations will please God. Prince Carnival's group likewise believes worship is a human activity, but one that must excite and invigorate in order to fulfill. These two groups battle each other instead of remembering the Lord and gladly hearing His Word.

God's Work for You

Suppose an earthly father has a precious gift for his son. He says, "Meet with me for dinner. I have something to give you." The son will certainly obey! But even greater than his obedience, the son will benefit by receiving his father's gift.

In the same way, God commands us to worship for reasons greater than obedience. Christ already pleased God for you,[Th] fulfilling all the commandments in your place. Even though worship involves human responses such as prayer, praise, and offerings, these responses amount to very little when compared to the banquet of blessings that God offers for you in worship.

Precious Gifts

In worship God gives precious gifts to you, His precious child! God's powerful Word builds and strengthens your faith. Your Lord promises you eternal life. During worship Jesus serves you. He invites you to a banquet of bread and wine with His body and blood for the forgiveness of sins.[F]

For these reasons, be regular in worship,[S] but understand why you worship. Receive anew the benefits of Christ's death and resurrection for you. Don't mourn with Lady Lent. Don't party with Prince Carnival. Rather, hear the Word. Hold it sacred and gladly learn it. For in this Word God delivers to you the blessings of eternal life!

Today, everything seems to work against family harmony.[Tu] Promiscuity, divorce, rebellion, and "lack of time" all conspire to put the family out of tune. Yet think of the natural harmony that God created in family relationships. Parents bear and nurture their sons and daughters through childhood. Children grow up and prosper by the talents they inherit or learn from their parents. As parents age and their health fails, they count on the steady hands of their children to support them. Care goes from child to parent and from parent to child in a symphony of honor, love, and service.

While experimenting with stringed instruments, ancient musicians made a remarkable discovery. They found that the sounds of the strings complemented one another in natural, mathematical relationships. These natural relationships formed the basis of the musical scales and chords that musicians use to create harmony.

In the commandments God reveals the natural harmony He created for human relationships. He describes how human beings honor Him as their heavenly Father by living in harmony as members of a family.

Family Life

Natural rhythm should flow through each aspect of family life. For example, why do parents have jobs? To support and care for their families. Certainly God wants parents to enjoy their work. But if work grows more important than family harmony, something has gone terribly wrong. Children need their parents' love more than they need the "things" of life (though they don't always realize this). If you are a parent, God calls you to honor Him by caring for your family. If you are a child, much of who you are comes from your parents. God calls you to serve them and cherish them.[W]

Every family experiences discord. Growing children crave independence. Older adults lament losing their independence. Family members sin against each other, sometimes cruelly. When your heavenly Father says, "Honor your father and your mother," He does not say, "Give up on your own life." However, He does urge you to share your life with your family.

If your family fails to forgive each other and pray together, don't make excuses. Drop every distraction. Call your family together around the heavenly Father's Word. Live by the rhythm He sets.

Father above All

Throughout the Bible, but especially in the New Testament, God describes Himself as a Father.[Th] Our Creator established the order of the universe as well as the home.[F] Peace in family life begins with knowing His peace, which He makes known through His Son, Jesus.[S]

Jesus takes away the sins we commit against family members. He heals our broken hearts and restores relationships. Like the family pictured here, rejoice in the harmony that your heavenly Father provides through His Son, Jesus Christ. He will draw you together in a symphony of honor, service, and respect.

22

Gustav Adolph Spangenberg (1828–1891). *Luther in His Family Circle.*

Honor your father and your mother.

What does this mean? **We should fear and love God so that we do not despise or anger our parents and other authorities, but honor them, serve and obey them, love and cherish them.**

Meditations: Change Blessing Praise Request

M Read the article on page 22. Tu Ephesians 5:31–6:4. Reflect on God's teaching about family.

W Proverbs 4:1–9. What should a family crave more than wealth? Th Romans 8:12–17. How has God been a Father to you?

F Psalm 139:13–18. Describe God's design. S John 1:10–18. How has the Father revealed Himself?

英特纳雄耐尔就一定要实现

纪念无产阶级诗人、《国际歌》作者欧仁·鲍狄埃

Chinese School (19th century). *Eugene Pottier Writing 'The International'.*

You shall not murder.

What does this mean? We should fear and love God so that we do not hurt or harm our neighbor in his body, but help and support him in every physical need.

Meditations: Change Blessing Praise Request

^M Read the article on page 25. ^Tu Jeremiah 17:5–14. How can the heart be cured? ^W 1 Thessalonians 4:3–12. What is your ambition? ^Th Proverbs 6:16–22. What does the Lord detest? ^F Luke 1:39–50. Summarize how this passage describes the unborn. ^S John 10:7–18. Why has Jesus come?

I n contrast to the violent struggle promoted by envy, the Bible teaches, "You shall not murder." God urges us not to clench our fists in rage but to open our hands in kindness by helping and supporting life as His gift.

One of the great ironies of human anatomy is that a person's heart is about the size of his fist. Though our heart hides within our chest, our hands make our heart known.[Tu] For example, the picture of Eugene Pottier demonstrates the agility of the artist's hand. But his drawing of Pottier's clenched fist wrings out hidden intentions. The crushing force of those fingers would squeeze the life out of the people whom Pottier and the artist despise—capitalists and traditionalists who will not embrace their vision. The fingers tighten until the hearts of their enemies beat no more.

As you look at this picture, you may comfort yourself with the thought that the doctrines of communism collapsed at the end of the twentieth century. But before you relax too much, recognize that other deadly doctrines still threaten life today.

Deadly Doctrines

"Our cause is just," angry terrorists plead as they pound their fists. More than 40 terrorists organizations throughout the world continue to threaten our safety and well-being today.[W] Frustration and mistrust put weapons into the hands of those too weak to argue their cause or too lazy to work for peace.

"You have the right to die," say supporters of euthanasia. While the rest of the world struggles for life, liberty, and the pursuit of happiness, the right-to-die movement wants doctors to renounce their oath to "do no harm." Once doctors renounce their oath, should healthy people put their lives into such doctors' hands?[Th]

"My body, my choice," declares the pro-choice movement, an argument that on the surface seems completely reasonable. But look at the hands of those who practice abortion. They hold scalpels, saline injections, and surgical vacuums. They try to hide the fact that more than "my body" is involved. The body of a baby is at risk,[F] a baby who has no choice but depends on the hearts and hands of others.

Open Heart, Healing Hands

If you have balled your fist in anger, if your heart has harbored hatred for others, God can relax your fist. Through Christ He can fill your heart with compassion.

To the meek, the murderous, and the confused alike, Jesus Christ opens His hands in a gesture of compassion. As God's Son, He held the power of life and death over others. But He chose to give His life for them instead. The open, nail-pierced hands of Jesus show God's compassion for us. He who gave us the precious gift of life to begin with now gives us new life through the forgiveness of His Son.[S]

When Eugene Pottier wrote the lyrics for "The International" in 1871, he envisioned a just struggle of the oppressed working class against heartless nobility and wealth. Pottier longed for an international brotherhood of workers who would create a new life for themselves. But, instead, the communist doctrines to which he clung resulted in the most vicious reign of death ever seen. According to the Black Book of Communism, *between 1917 and 1991 the communist struggle for new life caused more than 100 million deaths.*

The man and woman in Boucher's painting *Lovers in the Park* look completely satisfied. Time seems of no consequence as the young man weaves flowers into his beloved's hair. But, suddenly, another woman walks by and steals the young man's attention.

Temptation often promises satisfaction. Satan, the world around us, and our sinful flesh tempt us constantly to stray from God's plan for us. Thankfully, God has not left us defenseless against temptation. His Son knows and understands the human condition. As a human, Jesus experienced temptation and overcame it through God's Word and Spirit.[Tu]

Created Male and Female

God made each of us either male or female.[W] He wants us to understand, appreciate, and live out our "maleness" or "femaleness" in lives dedicated to Him. For many, adulthood includes a lifelong marriage and raising children. Others find themselves best suited to the single life. But God plans for men and women, married or single, to complement, support, and respect one another.[Th]

Sexual purity can be compared to a river. A river gives life and brings pleasure, supporting and sustaining the lands through which it flows. But a river also destroys if it overflows its banks.

God designed you for life and pleasure. But in the commandments He tells you to respect life's boundaries lest you destroy yourself or others. Sexually transmitted diseases, pornography, and many divorces result from a flood of sexual sins. God expects you, married or single, to honor Him in your thoughts, words, and deeds.

Faithfulness and Fulfillment

By His Word and Spirit, God provides you with the same power that enabled Jesus to resist temptations.[F] By His Word and Spirit, you can enjoy a life that blesses instead of destroys. Find pleasure and satisfaction in honorable relationships, which God enables you to build.[S] God promises to remain faithful to you and bless you with faithfulness and fulfillment.

You shall not commit adultery.

What does this mean? We should fear and love God so that we lead a sexually pure and decent life in what we say and do, and husband and wife love and honor each other.

François Boucher (1703–1770). *Lovers in the Park.*

Meditations: Change Blessing Praise Request
^MRead the article on page 26. ^{Tu}Matthew 4:1–11. Note how Jesus resisted temptation.
^WGenesis 2:18–25. How did Eve complement Adam?
ThGenesis 39:1–10. Reflect on Joseph's sense of devotion. ^F1 Corinthians 10:6–13. What does God provide?
^SEphesians 5:21–33. How did Christ love the church?

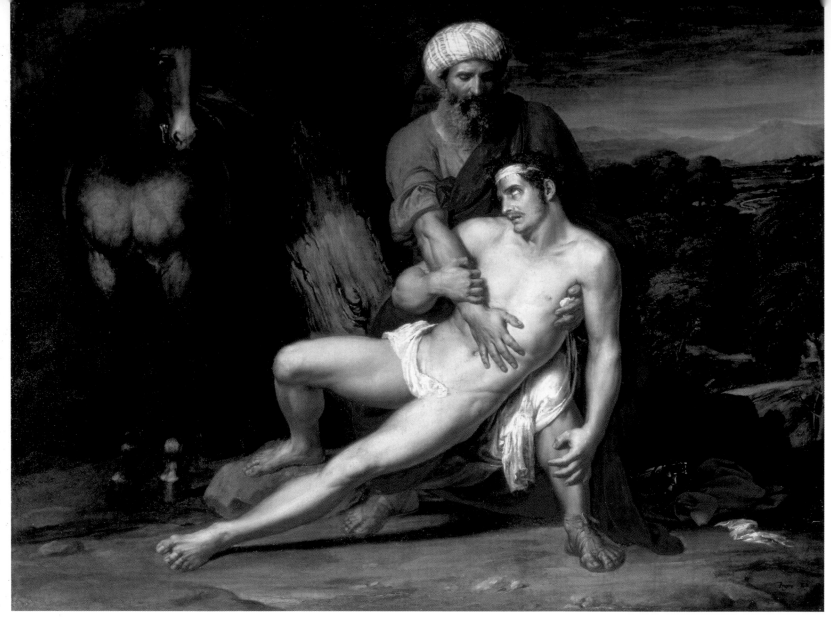

Rafael Tejeo (1798–1856). *The Good Samaritan.*

You shall not steal.

What does this mean? We should fear and love God so that we do not take our neighbor's money or possessions, or get them in any dishonest way, but help him to improve and protect his possessions and income.

Meditations: Change Blessing Praise Request
^MRead the article on page 29. ^{Tu}Genesis 14:8–16. Summarize Abram's heroism. ^WLuke 10:29–37. What motivated the Samaritan?
Th Galatians 5:13–18. How should Christians use their freedom? ^F2 Corinthians 8:8–15. What did Jesus become for your sake?
^SPsalm 146. Reflect on God's compassion.

A re you a hero?" the reporter asked, with the wreckage of the September 11th terrorist attacks smoldering in the background. "I was just doing my job," said the New York City firefighter. Police officers and Pentagon workers responded the same way. Though we call public workers by various titles, ultimately we call them to *be* heroes. We expect them to defend our property and us.

In the words "You shall not steal," God expects something heroic from you. As pictured here, God calls you to compassion. He calls you to act heroically by protecting the life, property, and income of others.[Tu]

Neighbors and Strangers

"Don't talk to strangers!" we tell our children. Sound advice. But as adults, we are commanded by God to abandon our own advice. He calls us to act compassionately toward neighbors and strangers alike.

Rafael Tejeo's *The Good Samaritan* illustrates a parable from Jesus about a stranger helping another stranger, a Samaritan helping a Jewish man. These two races despised each other. Yet this crisis left no room for discrimination. The Samaritan didn't need to know anything about the man who fell among thieves. He didn't need to know how old the man was, what he thought about Samaritans, or whether he could provide a reward. The man's wounds simply moved a stranger to compassion.[W]

The Compassion of Christ

Compassion is part of a Christian's job description.[Th] Just as firefighters and police officers are called to defend property and life, Christ calls us to care for the property and life of others. Just as public servants sometimes give up their lives for others, God may even call you to make the ultimate sacrifice by giving up your life.

When Jesus' disciples first heard the parable of the Good Samaritan, they did not comprehend its full meaning. Today, we can see Jesus' parable about compassion in light of His own sacrifices. Finding us stripped of our righteousness, Jesus took pity on us. He bandaged our wounds, provided for our healing, opened the treasures of heaven, and paid for our care. Jesus became poor so that we might become rich in God's righteousness, life, and peace.[F] Because of His compassion, we possess heaven.[S] Because of His ultimate sacrifice, we have the power to help others to care for all they are and possess.

The market choices of the storyteller Aesop provide us with keen insight. On one occasion Aesop's master ordered him to prepare a banquet for some special guests, instructing him to serve the finest meat. Surprisingly, Aesop served tongue! The master was outraged. But Aesop asked, "What is finer than the tongue? After all, with it we can speak and eat and sing."

At the next banquet the master tried to outsmart Aesop. He sent him to the marketplace for the worst meat, confident that this would cause Aesop to buy some choice cut. Again, Aesop served tongue. "What is worse than the tongue?" Aesop asked. "After all, with it so much pain is caused and so much harm done."

The Best and the Worst

Your tongue is a wonderful gift of God. With it you speak and sing, eat and swallow. Your tongue can defend, encourage, and explain everything in the kindest way. As demonstrated by this painting of a marketplace, people love to share news and ideas. They crave good conversation. Aesop had it right. What is finer than the tongue?

Yet what is worse than the tongue? Aesop had this right too. So does the artist. Look at the woman in the peach dress. So much gets whispered behind a hand. A tongue can betray a confidence, stretch the truth, gossip, and tell lies. Its words can devastate. As the apostle James complains, "No man can tame the tongue."[Tu]

Taming Your Tongue

By your own means, you will never force your tongue to repent. The Bible depicts people gnawing their tongues and clenching their teeth in agony rather than confessing their sins and receiving God's forgiveness.[W] Your tongue needs more than teeth and jaw to tame it. It needs the mind of Christ.[Th]

The prophet Isaiah says that Christ had no deceit in His mouth (53:9). The more that Christ is a part of your life, beginning with your mind and heart, the more honorable your tongue will be. Just as Jesus healed and loosed the tongue of the mute,[F] He will heal your tongue and loose it from the lies, betrayal, and slander that entrap it. The Lord will touch your mouth and fill it with His Word.[S] Forgiven of your sins, you will wish for a thousand tongues by which to thank and praise Him.

Paul Gauguin (1848–1903). *Ta Matete.*

You shall not give false testimony against your neighbor.

What does this mean? **We should fear and love God so that we do not tell lies about our neighbor, betray him, slander him, or hurt his reputation, but defend him, speak well of him, and explain everything in the kindest way.**

Meditations: Change Blessing Praise Request
MRead the article on page 30. TuJames 3:1–12. Summarize the damage done by the tongue.
WRevelation 16:7–11. What will the wicked say or not say? ThPhilippians 2:5–16. How will every tongue respond?
FMark 7:31–37. What did the mute tongue do? SJeremiah 1:4–10. Reflect on your calling.

You shall not covet your neighbor's house.

What does this mean? We should fear and love God so that we do not scheme to get our neighbor's inheritance or house, or get it in a way which only appears right, but help and be of service to him in keeping it.

You shall not covet your neighbor's wife, or his manservant or maidservant, his ox or donkey, or anything that belongs to your neighbor.

What does this mean? We should fear and love God so that we do not entice or force away our neighbor's wife, workers, or animals, or turn them against him, but urge them to stay and do their duty.

Hieronymus Bosch (c.1450 – 1516). *The Haywain*. c. 1500.

Meditations: Change Blessing Praise Request
^MRead the article on page 33. ^{Tu}1 Kings 21:2–19. Does God support ownership of personal property?
^WPsalm 23. How do you get what you want? ThPsalm 37:3–11. How does this psalm describe God's people?
^FRomans 7:7–25. What does God's Law reveal? ^SJames 4:1–10. What counsel does this passage have for you?

We talk about "Grasping at straws." The Dutch would say, "In the end, it's all hay." That's what the artist shows in his picture of a great hay wagon. The hay represents the cheap, common goods of this life for which everyone struggles, but which no one can hold onto.[Tu] The greedy hands of peasants and kings grab all they can get as the wagon rolls by, stirring sinful desires.

Desires

What do you want?[W] No doubt, you want what is yours and perhaps what belongs to another. Home, spouse, children, friends, business, and inheritance. To touch these possessions is to risk revenge, as the victims of the hay wagon discover.

Yet wanting and getting more is almost a religion, with millions of devout disciples. Like the people pictured here, we want what is ours—and ever more. Having more only leads to wanting more. We chase earthly goods and grope to sit on top of the pile. Is there ever an end to the cycle? Look again at the painting. You see the end under the wagon's crushing wheels.

Contentment in Christ

In contrast to the coveting pictured here, the Bible teaches, "Delight yourself in the LORD and He will give you the desires of your heart."[Th] God forbids coveting.[F] His cure for covetousness is contentment. Contentment comes from helping others enjoy what they have, even if it means caring enough only to compliment someone on her diamond earrings or his Rolex. Contentment can be seen among those willing to resolve a family or marital rift without using a lawyer and the courts. In the end, whatever we own and whatever we want succumbs to the old adage "You can't take it with you."

However, you do possess one thing that you will take with you. You received it as a gift from God your Father. Were you to lose everything you own, this one thing would remain: your faith in the One who gave His life to save you—Jesus. He stands above all things ready to bless you with forgiveness, life, and eternal salvation. Praise God for faith in Jesus. Use it to be happy with the blessings you have, but feel free to ask for more. Use that faith to help others enjoy and recognize the source of their blessings. "Delight yourself in the LORD and He will give you the desires of your heart" (Psalm 37:4).[S]

I n ancient and medieval times, farming required thousands of peasants. Today, a single farmer with a single tractor can exceed the output of multitudes of peasants. But despite vast changes in technology, the basic planting technique has remained the same since the time of Adam: prepare the field, then plant the seed.

The example of preparing and planting can help you understand how God works through His Word in your life.[Tu] Just as a farmer must first break the soil, God breaks your sinful heart with His Law. Just as a farmer sows seed into the ready soil, God plants His Gospel in your ready heart.[W] God has always worked this way in people's lives and will continue to work this way until the end of time when Christ returns.[Th]

Teamwork

The picture from a medieval calendar helps us understand how this sowing process of the Word of God works. It is a two-stage process. A cultivator, rugged and heavy, is necessary to break up the ground to provide openings for the seed to become embedded, take root, and grow. God's Word, the Bible, contains passages and even entire sections that work like a cultivator, breaking up the hardest of surfaces: stubborn human hearts. These sections are the Law of God. In His Law, God commands good works of thought, word, and deed, but He also convinces of sin and condemns. He prepares human hearts to receive life-giving seed.[F]

The cultivator is followed by the sower, the second stage in the sowing process of the Word of God. This seed is the Gospel sections of the Bible, all those passages that tell of God's grace and the Good News of salvation in Jesus Christ. In the Gospel, God freely gives forgiveness of sins and thereby scatters His seed in abundance. The Gospel is potent seed that takes root in people's lives. It grows faith, new life, and even the power to please God with good works.[S]

Law and Gospel

Each time you read the Bible, look for this two-stage work of God's Word. God's Law calls you to change from your sinful ways. The blessings of the Gospel make that change possible through Jesus Christ, your Savior. (See "Ways to Use *To All Eternity.*" Note that change [Law] and blessing [Gospel] are the first two steps in the devotional questions of this guide.)

What does God say about all these commandments?

He says: "I, the Lord your God, am a jealous God, punishing the children for the sin of the fathers to the third and fourth generation of those who hate Me, but showing love to a thousand generations of those who love Me and keep My commandments." [Exodus 20:5–6]

What does this mean?

God threatens to punish all who break these commandments. Therefore, we should fear His wrath and not do anything against them. But He promises grace and every blessing to all who keep these commandments. Therefore, we should also love and trust in Him and gladly do what He commands.

Limbourg Brothers (15th century). *October, Tres Riches Heures.*

Meditations: Change Blessing Praise Request

MRead the article on page 34. TuMark 4:1–9. Which type of soil are you?
WMark 4:13–20. What hinders you from receiving God's Word? ThIsaiah 55:6–13. Reflect on God's promise about His Word.
FMark 12:28–37. Summarize the teaching of the Law. SRomans 6:1–11. How does God give you new life?

Taddeo Gaddi (c.1300–1366). *Tree of Life (Tree of the Cross)*.

Meditations: Change Blessing Praise Request

^MRead the article on page 37. ^{Tu}Ezekiel 16:1–14. Reflect on the state of Jerusalem and God's loving care for her.

^WJohn 5:31–40. How does the Old Testament describe Jesus? ThIsaiah 52:13–53:12. Reflect on Isaiah's prophecy about the cross.

^FGalatians 3:1–9. What difference did the message of the cross make for the Galatians?

^SGalatians 3:10–18. Contrast the Law and the promise of the Gospel.

J effrey, it's time for supper!" his mother called.

Disappointed, Jeffrey walked away from the grove of orange trees where he played with his friend Matthew.

"You have to go in for supper!" Matthew teased. "I get to stay out as late as I want."

As Jeffrey walked home, his parents' rules frustrated him. Matthew's parents seemed so much cooler because they didn't call him away from play or have so many rules.

Later in life, Matthew and Jeffrey discussed this experience. To Jeffrey's surprise, Matthew said that he would have given anything for his mom to call him to supper— just once. Since Matthew's parents were alcoholics, they failed to watch out for him. Though they loved Matthew dearly, their vices hindered them from showing their love. Hearing this, Jeffrey saw his own parents differently. He saw more than their rules. He saw his parents' constant love and care.

More Than Rules

People often see Christianity and the Bible as nothing but rules—especially the Old Testament. Like Jeffrey, they fail to recognize the message beyond the rules: God's loving care.[Tu] Though the Bible certainly has rules, it also constantly proclaims God's loving care through the person and work of Jesus Christ.[W]

The painting *The Tree of Life* boldly illustrates this truth. The cross of Jesus sprouts branches of text. At the end of each branch appears the portrait of one of the Old Testament prophets who preached God's love and forgiveness through a coming Savior centuries before Jesus appeared.[Th] At the top and the bottom appear the four Gospel writers, pointing to Christ. The painting demonstrates that the message of God's love—the Gospel of Jesus Christ—runs throughout the Bible. The careful reader of the Bible constantly notes these two messages: God's Law (His rules) and the Gospel (the promise of forgiveness and new life through Jesus Christ).[F]

See Both Law and Gospel

As you read your Bible, look for both messages. No matter where you are in Scripture, if you find you don't understand what's going on, take note of God's rules and also look for God's promise of love and forgiveness. God's Law prepares you to hear about the love of Jesus. The Law helps you see how much you need a Savior.[S] What security comes from knowing you have a Lord who cares enough to admonish you!

Tree of Life

Your Lord loves you so much. He also freely grants you His grace and forgiveness. God's love is made certain to you in Jesus Christ. Whether you're a youth playing in an orange grove or a parent struggling to care for your children, remember and learn from the tree of life. Look to the cross to understand the great depth of God's love for you.

THE GOSPEL

the Apostles'

I believe in God,

the Father Almighty, Maker of heaven and earth.

P15 – 16
(102–107)

And in Jesus Christ,

His only Son, our Lord, who was conceived by the Holy Spirit, born of the Virgin Mary, suffered under Pontius Pilate, was crucified, died and was buried. He descended into hell.

The third day He rose again from the dead. He ascended into heaven and sits at the right hand of God, the Father Almighty.

From thence He will come to judge the living and the dead.

P 16–17
(119–14)

I believe in the Holy Spirit,

the holy Christian church, the communion of saints, the forgiveness of sins, the resurrection of the body, and the life everlasting.   Amen.

(147–173)

CREED

Resurrection

Holy

Trinity

The Trinity controversy involves much more than an ancient argument over a little Greek letter. It affects your salvation personally. The persons of the Trinity show God's work of salvation in your life.

The heavenly Father created you through Jesus Christ. Jesus Christ revealed the Father to you and sent His Holy Spirit. The Holy Spirit testifies about Jesus and makes you a partaker of the Father's holiness. These three are one true and eternal God, blessing you with everlasting salvation.

Paintings of the Trinity, such as the one you see here, often show the Son and the Father enthroned at eye level with each other. Amazingly, such careful positioning comes from an early church controversy involving a single letter of the Greek alphabet.

The controversy started when a minister named Arius taught that Jesus didn't always exist. Going against the Scriptures (Romans 9:5; Titus 2:11–14), Arius taught that the heavenly Father created Jesus.[Tu] For Arius, Jesus was *like* God but not truly God, equal with the Father.[W] When other ministers heard Arius's new teaching, they vigorously opposed it. Based on Scripture, they insisted that the Father, Son, and Holy Spirit have always existed and share the *same substance*.[Th] (The difference between the Greek words for *like* and *same substance* is one letter: an *i*.) These three persons are one true and eternal God.

Witnesses of the Trinity

Today, some historians criticize the early Christians for this debate about the relationship between the Father, Son, and Holy Spirit. They argue that the whole issue stemmed from philosophy and not from the Bible. Other religions also criticize the doctrine of the Trinity (*tri* meaning "3"; *unity* meaning "1"). They wonder how God can be three and one at the same time.

To understand the teaching about the Trinity, notice two people standing close to the Trinity in this painting: Mary and John the Baptist. In the New Testament, Mary was the first to hear about the persons of the Trinity. When the angel visited her, he said she would give birth to the "Son of God" through the Holy Spirit and the Most High.[F] Later, when Jesus came to John for baptism, John saw the heavens open. He heard the voice of the heavenly Father and saw the Holy Spirit descend as a dove upon Jesus.[S] Before Jesus ascended into heaven, He confirmed these testimonies, asking His disciples to baptize in the *name* (1) of the *Father*, *Son*, and *Holy Spirit* (3).

An example can help us begin to understand this profound mystery. Critics of the teaching about the Trinity argue that $1 + 1 + 1$ cannot equal 1. True. The doctrine of the Trinity does not add up by human reason. However, God's reason and eternal nature surpass our reason. Consider the following example from multiplication: $1 \times 1 \times 1$ does equal 1! Just as multiplication is a higher form of math than addition, God's teaching and eternal being are higher than our reason. Of course, this example cannot fully describe the true nature of the eternal God. But that's not the purpose of the teaching about the Trinity. In humility, this teaching simply tries to describe what God testifies about Himself in Scripture.

I believe in God.

Titian (c.1488–1576). *Adoration of the Trinity.*

Meditations: Change Blessing Praise Request

^MRead the article on page 40. ^{Tu}John 1:1–14. Who created all things?

^WPhilippians 2:5–11. Describe the relationship between the Father and the Son.

ThJohn 10:22–39. What did the Jewish people understand about the claims of Jesus?

^FLuke 1:26–38. Reflect on the angel's last words to Mary and the teaching about the Trinity.

^SMatthew 3:11–17. Reflect on your Baptism in God's name.

I believe in God,
the Father Almighty.

Honoré Daumier (1808–1879). *The Kiss, or A Man and His Child.*

Meditations: Change Blessing Praise Request
ᴹRead the article on page 43. ᵀᵘIsaiah 6:1–8. How does Isaiah respond? ᵂGalatians 4:1–7. What does the Spirit teach us to cry?
ᵀʰPsalm 85. What has righteousness to do with peace? ᶠEphesians 3:14–21. Why does the Father give you His Spirit?
ˢColossians 1:15–23. What is your relationship to Christ?

When naturalist William Beebe visited his friend Teddy Roosevelt at Sagamore Hill, they would go outside after sunset and gaze into the heavens. One would locate the spiral galaxy Andromeda, larger than our own galaxy, with 100 billion suns larger than our own. They would discuss the distance to Andromeda, 750,000 light years away. Then one would say, "Now we are small enough," and they would turn in for the night.

The greatness of the heavens humbles us. The mighty, spiraling galaxies proclaim just how small we are. Yet the Bible points to these galaxies for a greater purpose. It teaches that all the wonders of the universe proclaim the heavenly Father's loving care for us.

God Is Great

When we look at the heavens, we can only conclude that God is great. The Bible calls God "the Father Almighty" because all power in heaven and earth comes from Him. God is without beginning or end, all-knowing, present everywhere, and holy. Knowing this puts us in our place,[Tu] since we easily take God for granted or even behave as though we are the center of the universe. But God's greatness isn't the whole story. When the Bible celebrates God's power proclaimed by the universe, it also reminds us that the almighty God claims us as His children.[W]

God Is Good

Look at Daumier's picture of the man and the child. Notice the man's powerful arms and legs, his rolled-up sleeves, how easily he lifts the small child. These features alone might cause fear. What harm could such a powerful man do to such a defenseless child, especially if that child has done something wrong?

However, Daumier shows the man kissing the child—his child. That kiss completes the picture even as it completes our understanding of God. God's response to a fallen world was not to destroy it, but to prepare a great kiss.[Th] He now plants that kiss on our cheek and claims us as His children through the Gospel.[F]

We Thank Him

Many parents teach their children to pray at meals: "God is great, God is good, and we thank Him for our food." Like Beebe and Roosevelt, you need to proclaim the greatness of God. Yet you cannot see God's greatest work by looking into the sky.

Turn your eyes upon Jesus. See in His face the face of the almighty God who loves you and willingly gives His life for you. He claims you as His greatest work by taking away your sin and restoring you as His dear child.[S]

In 1735 and 1737 Carl Linnaeus published two famous works of science: *The System of Nature* and *The Types of Plants*. These two books carefully described how scientists could distinguish the varieties of life from one another. Today, students around the world continue to learn Linnaeus's system for studying life.

As Linnaeus studied thousands of plants and animals, he noticed how wonderfully nature fit together. What seemed disordered or confusing with simple observation became clear with careful observation.[Tu] For example, although breeding could radically change the appearance of a plant or animal, breeding did not change the species of a plant or animal. Linnaeus attributed this harmony and consistency in nature to the Maker of heaven and earth.[W]

According to Kind

Linnaeus found affirmation for his belief in natural harmony in the Book of Genesis, which describes God's orderly creation. He noted how God established "kinds" of animals and plants that reproduced one another ("kind" should not be confused with the modern scientific term "species"). Although variety flourished within each kind of life, antelopes remained antelopes and flowers remained flowers. The order established by God perpetuated itself from generation to generation.

However, Linnaeus's positive description of nature does have its limitations. Since the fall into sin, described by Genesis 3, careful observation of nature also reveals disharmony and destruction.[Th] The balance in creation tilts with self-destruction and disease. Nowhere is this more evident than among human beings!

Praise Your Maker

Thankfully, the Maker of heaven and earth has not left us to ourselves. The Bible teaches and the lives of countless people show that our Creator continues to care for His creation.[F] God demonstrates this care not only by providing for our physical needs. He also sent His Son, Jesus, to restore life and re-create us in His image: holy and righteous.[S]

Each time you see a beautiful tree, laugh at the antics of a pet, or enjoy a meal, remember your Maker. Offer thanks to Him for the order and harmony that He created and maintains for you. In Jesus' name, thank Him for the new life He offers.

Maker of heaven and earth

What does this mean? I believe that God has made me and all creatures; that He has given me my body and soul, eyes, ears, and all my members, my reason and all my senses, and still takes care of them.

He also gives me clothing and shoes, food and drink, house and home, wife and children, land, animals, and all I have. He richly and daily provides me with all that I need to support this body and life. He defends me against all danger and guards and protects me from all evil.

All this He does only out of fatherly, divine goodness and mercy, without any merit or worthiness in me. For all this it is my duty to thank and praise, serve and obey Him. This is most certainly true.

Master Bertram of Minden (c.1345–c.1415). *The Grabower Altar.*

Meditations: Change Blessing Praise Request
MRead the article on page 44. TuPsalm 8. Reflect on your place in creation.
WPsalm 104:14–23. Reflect on God's continuing role in creation. ThGenesis 3:14–24. Find your place in this passage.
FHebrews 1:1–12. How does this passage describe Jesus? SColossians 3:1–11. What has Christ restored/renewed in you?

And I believe in Jesus Christ, His only Son, our Lord, who was conceived by the Holy Spirit, born of the Virgin Mary.

What does this mean? I believe that Jesus Christ, true God, begotten of the Father from eternity, and also true man, born of the Virgin Mary, is my Lord.

Fra Angelico (1387–1455). *Annunciation.* (Detail.)

Meditations: Change Blessing Praise Request
MRead the article on page 47. TuMatthew 1:18–25. Why did God become man?
WHebrews 2:10–18. What experiences has Christ shared with sinners? Th1 John 1:1–7. Where does God "walk"?
FMatthew 4:12–17. What draws near with the light of Christ? SJohn 1:3–13. How has Christ revealed the Father?

The truth about light seems unbelievable. Light travels at more than 186,000 miles per second. It radiates from the sun as well as from a humble matchstick. When concentrated, light vaporizes most materials (via lasers). Yet it also transmits data, images, and the human voice over our phone lines (via fiber optics).

The truth about Jesus Christ also seems unbelievable. Especially the truth pictured here: His conception.[Tu] With a beam of light radiating from heaven and falling on the virgin Mary, the artist tries to express the truth that Jesus Christ is born of heaven and earth. He is both true God and true man.[W]

Light from Light

As the early Christians struggled to describe the incredible truth that Jesus is God, begotten of the Father eternally, they settled on a comparison with light.[Th] Jesus is like "Light of Light." Just as light constantly radiates from the sun, Jesus comes from the heavenly Father.

Yet Jesus was also born of the virgin Mary. How do we understand this? Inventions such as the oil lamp and the light bulb changed our relationship with light. They domesticated light so that it could serve among us. Jesus' conception and birth had a similar effect on our relationship with the Almighty. Jesus shares the Father's powerful essence yet humbly appeared on earth to serve us.

Mysterious Light

Since ancient times, scientists have struggled to understand the nature of light. In the nineteenth and twentieth centuries, scientists described light with comparisons, stating that it behaves like waves or like particles. Scientists have never been able to reconcile these two ways of talking about light. To this day the study continues.

Just as we cannot fully understand the truth about light, we cannot fully understand the truth about Jesus. The Bible does not try to explain Jesus, but describes His source and what Jesus has done for our salvation.[F] Jesus came from heaven in order to teach us about the heavenly Father.[S] He came to serve us by taking away our sins, dispelling the darkness that would shroud us. Before ascending into heaven, He promised to abide with us to all eternity.

The person sitting between death and life in the painting represents you and every person caught between the hope and despair that come with living in this broken world. There's a lot of pleasure to be had in life, but—let's face it—a lot of heartache too. And then, finally, we all come face-to-face with death.[Tu]

The problem is, our world is no longer the world God made in the beginning. The rebellion of our first parents injected death into God's perfect creation. In Adam, the very first man, all humankind was doomed to die.[W]

Bitter Consequences

Adam's sin has many bitter consequences for us all. Sadly, every day we confront them: guilt, shame, emotional or physical pain—all these stem from the sin of Adam and the rebellious heart we've inherited from him.[Th] You know the dilemma: set out to do the right thing and you end up doing the wrong thing. Sin happens. It comes naturally to everyone. But the price of that sin is quite unnatural: depression, loneliness, fear—these all stem from sin. Victims or perpetrators, it doesn't matter. Sin brings grim consequences to every man, woman, and child in this fallen world.

Worst of all, sin places all humankind under a curse. God's eternal justice decrees death to sinners. God warned Adam and Eve in the garden that if they rebelled, they would surely die. Die they did; and we've all been dying ever since. Not only that, but without God's intervention we would perish forever in hell. Such is Adam's legacy; paradise is lost, innocence is gone, and death has come to us all.[F]

Redeemed by Christ

But in the fullness of time, another "Adam" came along: God's own Son, yet one of us, our brother in human flesh. He was like us in every way, tempted just as we are, but with no sin of His own. Jesus Christ was so full of life He had to borrow sin in order to die. He took on the burden of our sins and carried all our sorrows, redeeming us from eternal death.

By His blood Christ has redeemed humankind from the tyrannical grip of sin, death, and hell. Sin and strife may still distress us from day to day, but by faith in Christ we already are cleansed from sin.[S] Jesus Christ has burst the bonds of death by His dying and rising again. He redeemed us by His blood to live again in hope, even though despair surrounds us.

In Holbein's painting, the Old Testament prophet Isaiah and the New Testament prophet John both point the lost and forlorn man to Jesus, the Lamb of God who takes away the sin of the world. They point to Jesus for you too. Thank God, He takes your sin away still today!

Hans Holbein the Younger (1497/98–1543). *Allegory of the Old and New Testaments.*

I believe in Jesus Christ, who suffered under Pontius Pilate

What does this mean? I believe in Jesus Christ, who has redeemed me, a lost and condemned person, purchased and won me from all sins, from death, and from the power of the devil.

Meditations: Change Blessing Praise Request

MRead the article on page 48. TPsalm 90:3–10. Why is death inevitable for every person?

WRomans 5:12–17. How did Adam's sin affect humankind? ThPsalm 51:1–6. Which comes first: the sins you do or the sinner you are?

FGenesis 3:1–8. Reflect on God's actions in the garden. S1 John 1:8–2:2. Describe Jesus' role in salvation.

Gustave Doré (1832–1883). *Christ Leaving the Praetorian.*

I believe in Jesus Christ, who was crucified, died and was buried. He descended into hell. The third day He rose again from the dead. He ascended into heaven and sits at the right hand of God, the Father Almighty.

What does this mean? I believe in Jesus Christ, who has redeemed me . . . not with gold or silver, but with His holy, precious blood and with His innocent suffering and death.

Meditations: Change Blessing Praise Request
MRead the article on page 51. TuMark 15:16–30. Reflect on Christ's humiliation. WIsaiah 7:10–14. How was Jesus' birth a humiliation?
ThPsalm 22:1–11. Reflect on Christ's trust. FActs 1:6–11. How and when will Jesus return?
SPsalm 130. Describe the redemption provided by Jesus.

With 11,674 steps that extend more than a mile, the service stairway for a special train in Spiez, Switzerland, stretches far beyond most stairways. It runs beside the special uphill track that makes the work of the train possible. When the train breaks down, some dedicated serviceman must climb these steps in order to restore the service.

The incredible painting on the opposite page reminds us of another set of remarkable steps: the steps Jesus took on His way to the cross. From the time Jesus descended from heaven to be conceived and born of the virgin Mary to the time He ascended back into heaven, He was taking the steps necessary to provide for your salvation.

Steps of Humiliation and Exaltation

In the painting of Christ leaving the Praetorium, our Savior descends the stairs, ready to take up His cross.[Tu] God came to us! Jesus is Immanuel (God with us).[W] He walks willingly to Calvary to suffer the death and hell we deserve because of our sin.[Th]

By His steps of humiliation (conceived, born, suffered, crucified, died, and buried), Jesus became one with us so that He might shoulder our burden. By His steps of exaltation (triumphed over hell, rose, ascended, seated at the Father's right hand, and coming again), Jesus removed the threat of death and punishment from us. He rose triumphant and victorious over sin, death, and hell. Then, after earning salvation for all people, He returned to the glorious throne from which He descended to be our Savior.[F]

Christ Still Serves You

As you consider this moment in your journey with the Lord, remember the many steps the Lord took for you![S] Though He grew tired and even stumbled in the journey beneath the awful weight of the cross, He continued to the journey's end for your salvation.

Today, Jesus still serves you. Though He has taken His place in glory, His greatest glory is to serve you. As you reflect on Jesus' incredible service, pray joyfully for His last step—His coming again in glory when you shall see Him face-to-face.

Jean-François Millet's art teacher considered him unteachable. People ridiculed Millet for choosing common peasant subjects rather than the "important" subjects chosen by established artists. Millet spent his life outside the centers of power, devoting himself to the ordinary.

Perhaps like the peasants that Millet painted, you consider yourself ordinary. Like the shepherdess in this painting, you may quietly live out your calling. But as you work and wait on the reappearing of your Savior, realize that God is pleased by *everything* you do in faith. Though critics may consider your work unimportant, your heavenly Father treasures you as a member of His kingdom serving in everlasting righteousness.[Tu]

Serve Your King

Rather than fretting over whether or not you have pleased God with your career choice or whether other people consider you important, rejoice that God blesses and honors all lawful occupations. He not only calls pastors. He also calls bankers, bookkeepers, students, homemakers, factory workers, doctors, farmers, and even sheepherders.[W]

Through your daily tasks, God gives you a place in which you continually serve Him. Everyday life forms the cathedral where you carry out the self-sacrificing work of Christ's "royal priesthood" and wait for the Lord's reappearing.[Th]

Wait on the Lord

Look at the shepherdess.[F] She stands amid her sheep, faithfully serving. But her eyes search for something more. Look at her place in the picture. Millet's peasants always stand like church steeples rising above the landscape, pointing toward something greater than themselves (see the painting on p. 72). They point toward eternity.

Though you may hold the most humble job by earthly standards, the Lord calls on you to point out the everlasting righteousness, innocence, and blessedness you enjoy as a servant of Jesus Christ. You serve in everlasting righteousness because God has declared you righteous through Jesus' death and resurrection. You serve in innocence, despite your sins, because Jesus traded your guilt for His innocence. You are blessed because your life's work shall end in your own resurrection with Jesus, who "lives and reigns to all eternity."[S]

Handwritten note (top left):
Lady taking care of earthly life (sheep), also looking towards glow in sky (God). This is like our responsibilities.

Also: we have to watch out for each other

I believe in Jesus Christ, who sits at the right hand of God, the Father Almighty. From thence He will come to judge the living and the dead.

What does this mean?
I believe in Jesus Christ, who has redeemed me that I may be His own and live under Him in His kingdom and serve Him in everlasting righteousness, innocence, and blessedness, just as He is risen from the dead, lives and reigns to all eternity. This is most certainly true.

Jean François Millet (1814–1875). *La Petite Bergere.*

Meditations: Change Blessing Praise Request
^MRead the article on page 52. ^{Tu}Romans 12:1–10. How do you serve fellow believers?
^WMark 6:1–6. How did Jesus serve God before He began to preach? Th1 Peter 2:4–12. Dignify your work.
^F2 Timothy 4:1–8. What should you long for? ^S1 Thessalonians 5:1–11. Contrast the ambitions of unbelievers and believers.

I believe in the Holy Spirit.

What does this mean? I believe that I cannot by my own reason or strength believe in Jesus Christ, my Lord, or come to Him; but the Holy Spirit has called me by the Gospel, enlightened me with His gifts, sanctified and kept me in the true faith.

Titian (c.1488–1576). *Pentecost.*

Meditations: Change Blessing Praise Request
MRead the article on page 55. TuColossians 1:3–14. From what has Christ delivered you?
W1 Corinthians 2:6–16. Without the Spirit, what can a person understand? ThJohn 16:5–15. What does the Spirit do?
FActs 2:1–11. What message did the Spirit cause the disciples to speak?
SRomans 8:1–11. Contrast the work of the sinful nature with the work of the Spirit.

When the first lamp ran out of fuel, Gary Lutes and his sons did not panic. After exploring caves for 26 years, Gary had never been lost. When the second lamp ran out, they grew nervous. They had foolishly left their emergency supplies behind and were having trouble finding them. When the third lamp ran out, total darkness encircled them. They could not move for fear of falling off some ledge. They could only hope that someone else would enter the cave and rescue them.

Spiritual darkness, like the darkness of a cave, makes it impossible to function.[Tu] Those in such darkness are hopelessly lost, even in comfortable surroundings. By their own reason or strength, they cannot move toward God or hope to please Him. Thank God that He enlightens us and keeps us in the faith by the work of the Holy Spirit.[W]

Enlightened by the Spirit

The total darkness of a cave is easily conquered. A single candle or even a struck match will always push back darkness into recesses and corners. Darkness is no match for light. This is also true spiritually.

Jesus poured light into our spiritually dark world when He sent the Holy Spirit.[Th] People who could only sit in darkness and despair because of sin and death have seen a great light. The Spirit, through the Word of God, Baptism, and the Lord's Supper, shines the light of Christ for you.

Light for God's People

Titian captures the Bible's story of the work of the Holy Spirit in his painting *Pentecost*.[F] Flames of light appear on the heads of the apostles while the Spirit fills the room with His presence and power. Darkness retreats.

Through His Holy Spirit, God continues to shine the light that overcomes darkness. Each time you open the Scriptures and read the Gospel, the Holy Spirit shines the light of the Gospel upon you. In this way He sanctifies and keeps you in the true faith.[S]

55

When Christopher Columbus first encountered the Caribbean Indians in 1492, he had mixed reactions. On the one hand, he had the mission and desire to share the Gospel with the Indians. On the other hand, he wondered whether such an unlearned, rude race was fully human and whether he could convert them.

If Columbus had reflected more on the teachings of the Christian faith, he would have had a ready answer for his dilemma. Conversion and sincere faith do not depend on education or race. Instead, the Holy Spirit calls all people by the Gospel into the Christian church.[Tu]

The Spirit Makes the Church

Like Christopher Columbus, the first Christians wondered about the conversion of other people. Being Jewish, they wondered whether the message of Christ's death and resurrection for the forgiveness of sins could hold the same blessings for other races. When persecution struck Jerusalem, a deacon named Philip traveled to Samaria. Philip preached to the Samaritans, and remarkably, crowds of foreigners believed his message.[W] The Holy Spirit called the Samaritans to faith just as the Spirit had called the Jewish people to faith.

Not long after this, the Holy Spirit encouraged the apostle Peter to visit the house of a Roman centurion named Cornelius. Arriving at the house, Peter found a crowd of Gentiles waiting to hear his message. When Peter proclaimed Christ to these Gentiles, the Holy Spirit called them to faith too.[Th] Peter immediately called for their Baptism into Christ and welcomed them as fellow members of the Christian church.

Through the Gospel

When you meet other people, take note of more than the color of their skin, the nation of their birth, or the state of their education. See them as people loved by Christ. Remember that the Holy Spirit desires to gather them into the Lord's kingdom through the Gospel.[F]

As the above examples demonstrate, the power of the Gospel does not dwell in the ability of the person proclaiming it. Nor does the power of the Gospel stem from the worthiness of the people hearing it. The Holy Spirit of God calls, gathers, enlightens, and sanctifies people of every race and nation through the Gospel.[S] He gathers them together into the holy Christian church by the forgiveness of their sins just as surely as He has gathered and forgiven you in Christ.

Handwritten margin notes:

I believe in the Holy Spirit, the Holy Christian church, the Communion of Saints, the forgiveness of sins, the ressurrection of the body, and the life Everlasting. Amen

WDTM?
I believe that I cannot by my own reason of strength believe in Jesus Christ my Lord or come to him, but the Holy Spirit has called me by the Gospel, enlightened me with His gifts, sanctified and kept me in the one true Faith. In the same way also ve calls, gathers, enlightens and Sanctified the whole Christian church on earth, and keeps it w/ Jesus Christ in the one true faith. In this Christian Church He daily and richly forgives all my sins and the sins of all believers. On the last Day He will raise me and all the dead, and give eternal life to me and

John Vanderlyn (1775–1852). *The Landing of Columbus.*

I believe in the Holy Spirit, the holy Christian church, the communion of saints, the forgiveness of sins.

What does this mean? The Holy Spirit has called me by the Gospel. In the same way He calls, gathers, enlightens, and sanctifies the whole Christian church on earth, and keeps it with Jesus Christ in the one true faith. In this Christian church He daily and richly forgives all my sins and the sins of all believers.

Meditations: Change Blessing Praise Request
MRead the article on page 56. TuJohn 3:1–8. What does the Spirit do? WActs 8:4–13. How did the Samaritans come to faith? ThActs 10:34–44. How did God bring the Gentiles to faith? FActs 2:42–47. Reflect on the activities of the earliest Christians. SRomans 10:8–18. With what tools does God create faith?

all believers in Christ. This is most certainly true.

Victor-Louis Mottez (1809–1897). *The Resurrection of the Dead.*

I believe in the Holy Spirit, the resurrection of the body, and the life everlasting. Amen.

What does this mean? On the Last Day He will raise me and all the dead, and give eternal life to me and all believers in Christ. This is most certainly true.

Meditations: Change Blessing Praise Request
^M Read the article on page 59. ^Tu Acts 17:24–34. What counsel did Paul offer?
^W 1 Corinthians 15:12–20. What makes the resurrection certain? ^Th 1 Thessalonians 4:13–5:3. What will happen when Christ returns?
^F Revelation 20:11–21:5. Contrast the end for the righteous and the unrighteous.
^S Revelation 22:12–21. What do the Spirit and the church cry out?

hen I look forward and hope we may all be together . . . ," wrote scientist Oswald Avery to his brother Roy, "and living out our days in peace." In this early-morning letter, Avery described the most noteworthy discovery of his scientific career: the proteins of DNA bear the genetic information upon which all life is based. Today, scientists continue to build on the hope first realized by Avery's discovery, the hope to restore and improve human life.

The hope to restore and improve human life filled the apostle Paul when he addressed the learned men of Athens.[Tu] The Athenians listened thoughtfully to Paul's words about God until he came to the message of the resurrection of the body, as pictured here. When Paul mentioned the resurrection of the body, many scoffed and refused to hear more. They refused to believe that God would restore the body in the resurrection on the Last Day.[W]

The Resurrection

Across the centuries, people have continued to attack the Christian belief in the resurrection of the body.[Th] Until recently, scientists rejected the idea that a dead body could be restored. Avery's discovery of DNA has reopened the discussion of the resurrection with a new twist. Scientists now know that all the information necessary to grow and develop a body can be found in a single microscopic cell.

People who formerly might have ridiculed the resurrection of the body could now reason, "If a scientist can restore the body of an animal using DNA, certainly the Maker of heaven and earth can restore the bodies of believers in the resurrection!" What seemed impossible before Avery's discovery now seems wholly reasonable.

Wholeness in Christ

Jesus' teaching of the resurrection is more than a point of argument or speculation. By this teaching Jesus offers us the promise of wholeness in salvation. He came to restore people in their entirety—body and soul—so that whole people may be together with Him on that Last Day.[F]

Oswald Avery's hope that his family might "all be together" enjoying peace finds certain fulfillment in Jesus' promise of the resurrection of the body and eternal life. In the resurrection, Jesus will raise up everyone from the darkness of death and restore all who trust in Him for heaven's eternal peace.[S]

In the mid 1980s the discoveries of Dr. Elizabeth H. Blackburn caused many scientists to rejoice. Previously, scientists believed that cells could only live so long and then had to die. Blackburn found that the enzyme telomerase could extend the life of cells. Her discoveries opened the possibility of doubling or tripling the human life span. Scientists around the world rejoiced over Blackburn's work and the hope it held for the future.

Christians, too, have a hope that causes them to rejoice. But this hope extends beyond the boundaries of earthly life. Because of the resurrection of Jesus and His promise to come again, we hope to enjoy eternity with God and the angels of heaven.[Tu]

Eternity in Heaven

Traditional depictions of eternal life often show quiet, angelic figures seated on clouds, piously strumming harps. Such pictures have their root in the Bible, but hardly do justice to what the Bible says. The Bible describes eternal life as a feast, a holiday banquet packed with joyful participants and activity.[W]

The artist Ferrari pictured angels as part of a heavenly band, undoubtedly singing praise to God. We might imagine angels in such a performance when they're not busy protecting us and fighting spiritual battles on our behalf. But a chief activity of angels and believers in heaven is praising God and rejoicing. If angels were human, we might call them "party people." For example, Luke tells us that heaven throws a party whenever someone comes to faith or returns to faith.[Th]

Christians rejoice about eternal life in heaven. But we must not diminish the importance of life as we live it now. While we may wonder exactly what life beyond death is like, we cannot waste time daydreaming of better days. God calls us to celebrate the days we have now by sharing the Gospel with others. We need to give those musical angels more cause to rejoice!

Joy Everlasting

God wants you to enjoy life on earth. But if scientists rejoice over the thought of extending earthly life, how much more should you rejoice over the blessings of eternal life with the Lord and His angels in heaven![F] Rather than basking lazily in God's gift of eternal life, rejoice with others. Tell them that God sent Jesus to do everything necessary to earn eternal life for all people.

You may never be rich and famous. You may never enjoy perfect health. You may never own a Ferrari. But the angels of heaven praise God for you, and they're waiting to party with you in person.[S]

Gaudenzio Ferrari (1475–1546). *Musical Angels.*

I believe in the Holy Spirit and the life everlasting. Amen.

What does this mean? **On the Last Day He will raise me and all the dead, and give eternal life to me and all believers in Christ. This is most certainly true.**

Meditations: Change Blessing Praise Request
MRead the article on page 60. TuRevelation 7:9–17. Describe how worship takes place in heaven.
WRevelation 19:1–9. What do God's people celebrate? ThLuke 15:1–10. Why do the angels celebrate?
FPsalm 16. What does God give in heaven? SPsalm 103:11–22. Whom does the psalmist command to rejoice?

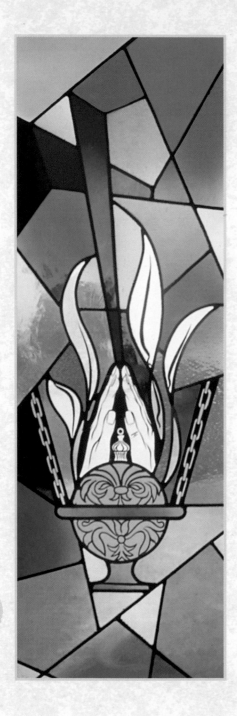

the **LORD'S**

Our Father

Daily Bread

Kingdom Forever

Glory

PRAYER

who art in heaven. 19 , 180

Hallowed be Thy name. 19 , 181-183

Thy kingdom come. 19-20,

Thy will be done on earth as it is in heaven. 20

Give us this day our daily bread; 20-21

and forgive us our trespasses

    as we forgive those who trespass against us; } 21

and lead us not into temptation, 21-22

    but deliver us from evil. 22

For Thine is the kingdom

    and the power and the glory forever and ever. Amen. } 22

Hallowed be Thy name

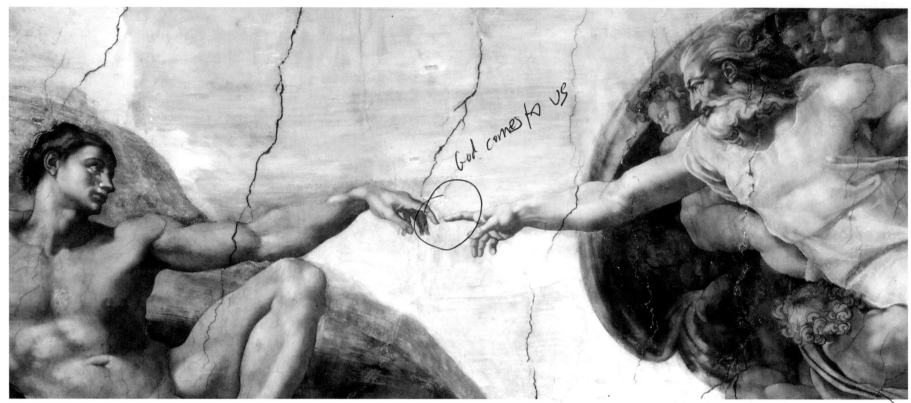

Michelangelo (1475–1564). *The Creation of Adam.* (Detail.)

Our Father who art in heaven.

What does this mean? **With these words God tenderly invites us to believe that He is our true Father and that we are His true children, so that with all boldness and confidence we may ask Him as dear children ask their dear father.**

Meditations: Change Blessing Praise Request
MRead the article on page 65. TuMatthew 6:5–15. How does the heavenly Father affect the practice of prayer?
WActs 17:22–31. Why did God create and order the universe? ThMatthew 11:25–30. What pleases the heavenly Father?
FPsalm 121. Reflect on God's activity. SLuke 11:5–13. What does the Father promise through Christ?

How do I pray when I don't believe in God?" asked a participant on an Internet bulletin board. "What I want to say is that I know the word 'praying' only in connection with 'praying to God'—thereby believing in a higher being to pray to. Since I don't believe in a higher being, I don't pray. But I think, I contemplate, I reason, I question, I wish, and I hope. Maybe that is praying in a sense—it's just not directed toward anybody."

The subject of prayer confuses many people. They see prayer as a means to search for answers or to improve their circumstances or attitudes. In contrast to all these ideas, Jesus invites us to understand prayer differently. For Jesus, prayer is first and foremost about whom you pray to: your Father in heaven.[Tu]

Created for Prayer

In Michelangelo's famous *The Creation of Adam*, the heavenly Father reaches out to Adam so that Adam might reach back to Him.[W] Prayer begins with God. He invites us to call Him "our Father." The focus of prayer begins our relationship to the Creator. He wants us to call on Him as more than some impersonal universal force or higher being.

Certainly God is a higher being. We confess the triune God as Creator of the heavens and the earth, all the stars and the vastness of space. With a single word He called creation into existence. For this and more we call Him almighty. Yet this great and awesome Creator stoops down and whispers to us, "Call Me your Father."

His Children

Simply put, it is because of Jesus that we call almighty God our Father. We are His children, invited by Him to reach for Him as often as a young child reaches for mommy or daddy.[Th] Yet, in contrast to the arms of any earthly parent, our heavenly Father never tires.[F]

Abba

Your Father in heaven hears every one of your prayers brought to Him in the name of His Son. He promises to answer every one of those prayers. He promises to answer according to His will, keeping your very best interests at heart.[S] After all, He created you. He paid a dear price for you. You are His child, with whom He is well pleased.

We pray so we can connect w/ God and he likes that because he loves us.

65

When God revealed Himself to Moses in the burning bush, Moses removed his sandals in God's presence. Realizing his sinfulness, he also hid his face "because he was afraid to look at God."[Tu]

God's Holy Presence

Sinners cannot hope to approach God without fear of His wrath and condemnation. For this reason, God does not demand that you come to Him. Rather, God has chosen to come to you. In the Old Testament, God appeared to Moses in a burning bush. But in the New Testament, God veiled His holiness and His divinity in the human body of Jesus Christ.[W]

Because of Jesus, you no longer need to fear the presence of God as Moses did. Like a rescuer using his body to shield a child from a burning house, Jesus' holy and perfect body shields and protects you from the fiery condemnation that you would experience on account of your sin.[Th] God now declares you sinless and holy for the sake of the risen Christ. He protects you so that "in Him and through faith in Him [you] may approach God with freedom and confidence" (Ephesians 3:12).

Holy People Living Holy Lives

When Christians pray, "Hallowed be Thy name," they pray that God's protection through Christ would never leave them and that His holiness would produce the fruits of holiness in their lives. Through their words and deeds, Christians carry Christ's presence into a lost and dying world.[F]

In Christ you have nothing to fear! You need not hide your face from God as Moses did, because Christ has forgiven all your sins and declared you holy. Likewise, you need not fear any enemy that opposes you: not sin, not death, and not hell. Christ has already defeated these unholy things for you! What remains? God's protection and precious promises.[S]

Raphael (1483–1520). *Moses and the Burning Bush.*

Hallowed be Thy name.

What does this mean? God's name is certainly holy in itself, but we pray in this petition that it may be kept holy among us also.

How is God's name kept holy? God's name is kept holy when the Word of God is taught in its truth and purity, and we, as the children of God, also lead holy lives according to it. Help us to do this, dear Father in heaven! But anyone who teaches or lives contrary to God's Word profanes the name of God among us. Protect us from this, heavenly Father!

Meditations: Change Blessing Praise Request
MRead the article on page 66. TuExodus 3:1–6. Reflect on what Moses saw and heard.
WHebrews 12:18–29. How are things different since Christ has come? Th1 Peter 2:19–25. What is the result of Jesus' sacrifice?
F1 Peter 1:6–16. What standard does God call us to uphold? S2 Peter 1:4–11. What flows from faith?

looks like Last Day →

Peter Paul Rubens (1577–1640). *The Defeat of Sannacherib, King of Assur.*

Thy kingdom come.

What does this mean? The kingdom of God certainly comes by itself without our prayer, but we pray in this petition that it may come to us also.

Jerusalem destroyed 571 BC

How does God's kingdom come? God's kingdom comes when our heavenly Father gives us His Holy Spirit, so that by His grace we believe His holy Word and lead godly lives here in time and there in eternity.

Meditations: Change Blessing Praise Request
M Read the article on page 69. Tu Revelation 12:1–12. How do God's people overcome? W Ephesians 6:10–18. Summarize how God equips you.
Th 2 Kings 18:26–37. How does the battle begin? F Isaiah 37:21–37. What does the Word of the Lord accomplish?
S Matthew 16:13–20. On what confession is the church, God's kingdom, built?

T wo armies clash. The battle continues day-by-day. The great struggle between good and evil—between God's kingdom and Satan's kingdom—continually swirls about God's church. The Bible teaches that the battle between good and evil will continue on two fronts till the end of time.

battle in us – temptation

We easily recognize the first front of this battle, the struggle for right and wrong played out before our eyes. However, we often live unaware of the second front, the spiritual battle for our souls, vividly described by Scripture.[Tu] On both fronts God's people wrestle not only against flesh and blood but also against spiritual enemies. Our heavenly Father sustains us in this battle through His Word.[W]

Sustained by the Word

Rubens's dramatic painting depicts the effects of God's Word and prayer in the lives of God's people. Sennacherib, King of Assyria, had attacked and captured all the fortified cities of the kingdom of Judah. He marched his army on Jerusalem, the home of God's Old Testament people. Hoping to avoid war, King Hezekiah of Judah gave Sennacherib all the gold in Judah. But he surrounded Jerusalem and demanded unconditional surrender. At the same time, Sennacherib blasphemed God.[Th] Encouraged by God's Word, Hezekiah turned to the Lord in prayer, asking the Ruler of heaven and earth to intervene.

In answer to Hezekiah's prayer, God promised deliverance for His people and condemned the king of Assyria. God's angel descended into the Assyrian camp to fight. Flesh and blood could not compete with God's angel. When the Judeans arose the next morning to view their enemies, they saw only corpses, tens of thousands of corpses left behind by Sennacherib as he fled.[F]

God's Victorious Kingdom

Rubens's painting provides not only a captivating picture of the battle with the Assyrians. It also portrays the ultimate outcome of the great struggle between good and evil. Wicked people and even the devil himself cannot compete with the Lord. As you face struggles and persecution, remember that the Lord fights for you. By His Word and Spirit, He sustains you for whatever the day may bring.

Jesus promises that not even the gates of hell can prevail against God's church, His kingdom.[S] This is first and foremost true of Jesus Himself, who has provided final and total victory through His death and resurrection. Like Hezekiah, boldly call on the Lord who reigns over all kingdoms of heaven and earth. He will sustain you and give you victory.

By the end of the first year in the Plymouth Colony, half of the men had died, as had 14 of the 19 women. Food supplies remained low. Sickness hindered improvement of the colony. Yet when the Mayflower returned to England in 1621, not one of the colonists went back. Instead they entrusted their lives to God's will in a new world.

Thomas Hart Benton's painting shows both the anxiety and the trust of the Pilgrims as they watched the Mayflower withdraw. No doubt they felt suddenly alone. Surely the new world held adventure and opportunity. But the world also held dangers, trials, and uncertainties. By faith they determined to found a "city on a hill," where God's will would be done on earth as it is in heaven.[Tu]

A Battle of Wills

Those of us who believe in Jesus face the threat of a host of enemies that would lead us to abandon God's will in our lives. God warns us to be wary of the devil's unrelenting tactics.[W] Sometimes we struggle when our own will conflicts with God's plan and direction. At other times, those around us prove an unhelpful—even a negative—influence.

Jesus knew God's will to save us from our sins.[Th] Yet He struggled as He talked with His Father. He prayed that God's will would be done.[F] And He prayed alone, without the aid and support of His closest friends. In the end He entrusted His life to His Father's hands and gained eternal life for us all.

To Build a Life

Each believer seeks to build a new life. In God's Word and Sacraments, we receive direction and power as we wrestle against all that would lead us away from God and the free gift of eternal life. Benton's depiction of the Pilgrims and their guns illustrates various approaches to preparing to do battle against evil. One Pilgrim kneels in prayer with a musket on his knee. A second Pilgrim kneels as if in prayer, one hand clutching his weapon. And a third stands watchful and ready, holding his gun as if ready to shoot.[S]

In a similar way, God's Spirit brings us to various states of readiness and action when we pray "Thy will be done." Even during those times when we feel uncertain or lacking in direction regarding an issue about which Scripture does not directly speak, we can pray with boldness and confidence, knowing that in all things God works good for those who love Him. Nothing will be able to separate us from His love for us in Christ Jesus our Lord.

Thy will be done on earth as it is in heaven.

What does this mean? The good and gracious will of God is done even without our prayer, but we pray in this petition that it may be done among us also.

How is God's will done? God's will is done when He breaks and hinders every evil plan and purpose of the devil, the world, and our sinful nature, which do not want us to hallow God's name or let His kingdom come; and when He strengthens and keeps us firm in His Word and faith until we die. This is His good and gracious will.

Thomas Hart Benton (1899–1975). *Prayer.*

Meditations: Change Blessing Praise Request

MRead the article on page 70. TuMatthew 5:1–16. Describe those who know and do God's will.

W1 Peter 5:1–11. Cite evidence of the devil's prowling in your life. Th1 Timothy 2:1–10. What does God want?

FLuke 22:39–46. Reflect on the intensity of Jesus' prayer.

SNehemiah 4:7–20. How does this story and the story of the pilgrims encourage you?

Steeple on church →

at sunset, ending their work

they are praying, they are grateful

Jean Francois Millet (1814–1875). *The Angelus.*

Give us this day our daily bread.

What does this mean? God certainly gives daily bread to everyone without our prayers, even to all evil people, but we pray in this petition that God would lead us to realize this and to receive our daily bread with thanksgiving.

What is meant by daily bread? Daily bread includes everything that has to do with the support and needs of the body, such as food, drink, clothing, shoes, house, home, land, animals, money, goods, a devout husband or wife, devout children, devout workers, devout and faithful rulers, good government, good weather, peace, health, self-control, good reputation, good friends, faithful neighbors, and the like.

Meditations: Change Blessing Praise Request
MRead the article on page 73. TuMatthew 6:25–34. What worries can you leave with the Lord today?
WGenesis 2:8–17. How did God provide for Adam and Eve before the fall into sin?
ThGenesis 8:15–22. How did Noah respond to God's provision? FExodus 16:10–18. What did the bread and meat teach the Israelites?
SLuke 1:46–55. Reflect on Mary's thanks to God for His greatest gift.

Jean Francois Millet's *The Angelus* suggests ample reason for thanking and praising God. The farmers pause to thank God during their harvest. The church bells at the end of the day remind them to pray and praise God for the birth of Jesus and all God's blessings (*Angelus* refers to the words spoken by the angel to Mary in Luke 1:28). They express sincere thanks for the daily care that God has shown them.[Tu]

Daily Bread

God has a history of richly supplying earth's people. In the Garden of Eden, replete with the best of every good gift, God arranged for the proper nurture of the first couple. He continued His care even after their disobedience.[W] Many years later, Noah's "daily bread" included plentiful timber from which to fashion the world's largest lifeboat.[Th] Later on, we read about God's people wandering through the wilderness, their hunger satisfied by daily "take-outs" of manna.[F] In each case, God's supply was enough.

Sometimes we pray carelessly or even forget to thank God at meals. We ramble routinely through mostly familiar words, not stopping to think about the inclusiveness of words like "Give us this day our daily bread." At times our "bread" comes in big loaves; other times we get the heel of a loaf. But, thank God, it is enough.

Daily Thanks

When we suffer some loss, we're tempted to think that we have less for which to be thankful. That's why we must never forget God's greatest gift, the gift remembered by these farmers as they pray among the potatoes.[S] The Holy Spirit delivered it, wrapped in cloth, while angels in the highest and shepherds in the lowest celebrated. Even better, the Spirit personalized the gift for you by providing the faith you need to know and accept this gift as your Savior! Possessing the Savior means life after death in the presence of God.

Having faith and salvation has implications. We who have it must give it away. We must share it with others. We must credit God for its priceless value. When we do that, we also experience something new. Our gift doesn't disappear when we give it away. People who know Jesus as their Savior always have enough.

We don't know her name. We do know her sin. "Caught in the act of adultery," her accusers said. They brought her to Jesus, hoping to trick Him: "In the Law Moses commanded us to stone such women. Now what do You say?" Jesus ignored them, calmly writing on the ground with His finger. When they pressed Him, Jesus straightened up and said, "If any one of you is without sin, let him be the first to throw a stone at her."[Tu] One by one the woman's accusers drifted away, conscience-stricken.

Of all the sons and daughters of Eve, Jesus alone was born without a tainted, sinful heart. In all His words and deeds, never once did Jesus violate the holy Law of God, His Father. Though He was tempted in every way just as we are, He remained always without sin.[W] Jesus could have cast the first stone against the condemned sinner who stood cowering before Him. But He did not.

Jesus Steps In

Cranach captures the dramatic moment of Jesus' intervention. Notice how Jesus boldly steps in front of the woman; His body stands as a shield against her accusers. Note their vile expressions, brute-like and near demonic. Note how innocent and pure the woman appears under Jesus' protection.

What Jesus did for this woman, He does for every contrite sinner. Jesus Christ frees broken hearts from sin and death. He was made to be sin for us, even though He had no sin of His own, that sinners might stand absolved and innocent, free from accusation and blame.[Th] He places His own flesh and blood between sinners and the just penalty of their sin.[F] Now, by faith in His blood, sinners stand before God innocent and pure, clothed in the very innocence and purity of God's own beloved Son.

All by Grace

Therefore, in Jesus' name sinners may stand fast and boldly pray to a loving Father in heaven despite their sin.[S] The forgiveness of sins is at the heart and center of the Christian life, thanks to the intervention of God's sinless Son. Whenever the devil charges, "You are a sinner," Christ Jesus has a different word. "I reverse that. I will be the sinner; by God's grace you shall go free."

Lucas Cranach the Elder (1472–1553). *Christ and the Woman Taken in Adultery.*

Martin Luther: 1483–1546 (handwritten)

Born Nov 10 (handwritten)
Died Feb 18 (handwritten)

And forgive us our trespasses as we forgive those who trespass against us.

What does this mean? **We pray in this petition that our Father in heaven would not look at our sins, or deny our prayer because of them. We are neither worthy of the things for which we pray, nor have we deserved them, but we ask that He would give them all to us by grace, for we daily sin much and surely deserve nothing but punishment. So we too will sincerely forgive and gladly do good to those who sin against us.**

Meditations: Change Blessing Praise Request

ᴹRead the article on page 74. ᵀᵘJohn 8:1–11. Reflect on accusations you have recently made.

ᵂHebrews 4:14–5:7. How has Jesus' sinlessness affected our prayers?

ᵀʰ2 Corinthians 5:11–21. What did Christ exchange with us (what did He become for us)?

ᶠRomans 3:19–26. How has the heavenly Father "presented" Jesus? ˢLuke 18:9–14. Contrast the "standing" of these two men.

**And lead us not
into temptation.**

What does this mean?
God tempts no one. We
pray in this petition that
God would guard and
keep us so that the devil,
the world, and our sinful
nature may not deceive us
or mislead us into false
belief, despair, and other
great shame and vice.
Although we are attacked
by these things, we pray
that we may finally
overcome them and win
the victory.

Piero di Cosimo (1462–1521). *Simonetta Vespucci.*

(Satan) temptation

Meditations: Change Blessing Praise Request
^MRead the article on page 77. ^{Tu}Genesis 3:1–6. Why was this fruit so tempting for Eve?
^W1 Peter 5:8–14. What promises does God attach to this warning?
ThLuke 4:1–13. Consider verses 8 and 12 in view of the fact that Jesus Himself is true God.
^FRevelation 20:11–21:4. How will the Lord clothe the church at the end of time?
^SLuke 22:24–32. Reflect on Jesus' answer to the tempter.

The most beautiful woman. The icon of social life in the most important city. The face sought by the men who changed the world.

Fifteen years after her death, painters still regarded Simonetta as the most beautiful of women. When she won a beauty contest in 1469, she took her place at the center of Florentine life. She enjoyed all the wealth and excitement of the city. She married Amerigo Vespucci, the man who would later give his name (America) to continents of the Western Hemisphere.

But at the age of 23, Simonetta died from a brief struggle with tuberculosis. She seemed to have everything. She lost everything. Piero di Cosimo painted Simonetta depicting Eve, encircled with temptation in the form of a serpent. She stands between a landscape of life and death. How fitting that the painter chose Simonetta as his model for the woman who truly lost everything: Eve, the first woman. Eve lost everything to temptation.[Tu]

Losing Everything

Our first parents, Adam and Eve, had everything they could ever want. Most important was their communion with God and immortality. Satan deceived them into believing that God had provided all they needed except for one thing: wisdom that would come from the tree in the middle of the garden.

Satan is the father of all lies. He tricked our first parents. He distorted God's Word. The world has been suffering ever since. Although Satan is our defeated enemy, he is still an enemy. He still seeks to lead God's children astray.[W] If you have faith in Jesus Christ as your Lord and Savior, you're Satan's target.

Satan tries to take us to Hell because he is afraid to go there and he will takes us w/ him.

Cling to the Word

Satan fears the Word because he knows that God's Word wields more than enough power to defeat any of his temptations. Jesus defeated the tempter in the wilderness by counter-striking the foe with God's Word.[Th] In the Word of God we gather our strength for our walk with Christ. The world's temptations—fueled by the evil foe—are to get us thinking that church and the Bible are not enough to have complete fulfillment. There must be fame, riches, or material possessions to say you've reached the top. But in the end, all of those objects disappear. All that is left is the sinner standing naked before the Creator.[F]

Every temptation we have faced has already been conquered through Christ. With His Word—the very Spirit working in our hearts—we can overcome that which seeks to destroy us. We can even meet death with a certainty that is the world's envy— an eternal reunion with Jesus in heaven![S]

I n A.D. 258 Roman soldiers seized a Christian deacon named Lawrence and cast him on a searing gridiron because he disobeyed the emperor. According to legend, the local Roman ruler demanded that Lawrence gather and deliver to him all the treasure of the church. When government officials arrived at Lawrence's church expecting to receive gold and silver, they instead met a crowd of poor people. The Romans asked why this crowd had gathered, and Lawrence explained that they were the church's treasure, bought by the precious blood of Jesus.[Tu]

When Jesus taught His disciples to pray, He did not want them to focus on earthly treasures or possessions. Nor did He promise them blissful earthly life. Jesus taught His disciples to pray "deliver us from evil" because He wanted them to know that they, like faithful Lawrence, would face suffering.[W] Jesus wanted them to express in prayer their trust in God alone for deliverance from evil.

Evil Exists

Philosophers have debated about whether evil truly exists. Many have concluded that evil isn't real, but only the absence or lack of good. However, ordinary people know for certain that evil exists. Suffering, pain, and martyrdom are as active in our world today as the imaginations of foolish philosophers.

Jesus did not promise us an end to evil in this life. Instead, Jesus taught us to expect persecution for our faith. Though Christians of every generation can tell stories of times when God has delivered them from evil, they can also tell stories like that of Lawrence, stories of how God's people bravely suffered evil for the sake of the Savior.[Th]

Boldly Pray

When you face evil or persecution, boldly pray the prayer your Lord has taught you. In the words of the Lord's Prayer, entrust your body and soul, possessions and reputation to the Lord. He treasures your life and will care for you in your hour of need.[F]

Christ calls you today as a witness of the treasures of His kingdom. Whether He delivers you immediately or sustains you in the midst of your suffering, He will one day take you from this valley of sorrows to Himself in heaven.[S]

Francesco de Rosa, called Pacecco (1607–1656). *The Martyrdom of St. Lawrence.*

But deliver us from evil.

What does this mean? We pray in this petition, in summary, that our Father in heaven would rescue us from every evil of body and soul, possessions and reputation, and finally, when our last hour comes, give us a blessed end, and graciously take us from this valley of sorrow to Himself in heaven.

Meditations: Change Blessing Praise Request

MRead the article on page 78. Tu1 Peter 1:17–25. When did God plan to pay for your sins?

WJohn 16:25–33. How does Jesus comfort His disciples in the face of evil?

ThActs 14:19–28. What did Paul and Barnabus explain to the new believers? FMatthew 5:1–12. What belongs to you as a child of God?

SRevelation 21:9–21. Summarize the adornment of Christ's bride in heaven.

Giovanni Francesco Guercino (1591–1666). *The Incredulity of St. Thomas.*

For Thine is the kingdom and the power and the glory forever and ever. Amen.

What does this mean? This means that I should be certain that these petitions are pleasing to our Father in heaven, and are heard by Him; for He Himself has commanded us to pray in this way and has promised to hear us. Amen, amen means "yes, yes, it shall be so."

Meditations: Change Blessing Praise Request
M Read the article on page 81. Tu John 20:19–29. With whom can you share this message about life in Christ's name?
W Deuteronomy 27:15–28:6. Reflect on the use of "Amen" in worship. Th John 14:5–14. How has Jesus asked us to pray?
F 2 Corinthians 1:12–22. On what basis do Christians say "Amen"? S Philippians 4:2–9. What follows the prayers and meditations?

Some historians credit Missouri congressman William D. Vandiver with giving his state its nickname, "The Show Me State." In 1899, while attending a banquet in Philadelphia, Vandiver remarked—in jest—about Philadelphia's claim to greatness. "I am from Missouri," he said. "You have got to show me."

The congressman's insistence on proof would make perfect sense to the apostle Thomas, pictured here. Thomas stubbornly refused to believe that Jesus had risen from the dead. But then the risen Lord appeared to him, showed him His wounds, and said, "Blessed are those who have not seen and yet have believed."[Tu]

A Word of Faith

The word *amen* is a Hebrew word that means "This is true."[W] It has the same root as the Hebrew words for "trusting" and "believing." When Christians pray "Amen," they express faith and confidence in things they cannot see.

Prayer arises out of faith. Rather than insisting on proof, as Thomas and the congressman did, Christians can take the Lord at His Word. We can trust that when God promises to answer prayer,[Th] He will without doubt answer prayer!

You need not ever wonder if God hears and answers your prayers. Simply pray by faith in Jesus, making your requests known to God, and rest in the confidence that He will provide for all your needs for Christ's sake.[F]

A Word of Power

The "Amen," through which you express God-given faith and confidence in the One who has redeemed you, refocuses your attention from yourself to your God. The "Amen" summarizes your confidence in God's unfailing provisions: Amen! *Your* will be done, not mine. Amen! *Your* kingdom come, not mine.

Do not let your sins keep you from prayer, and do not wonder if God will reject your prayers because of your weakness. In fact, completely ignore your own unworthiness! Pray confidently in the name of Jesus,[S] clinging to the powerful "Amen" and trusting that your God truly is faithful and will answer all your prayers for the sake of Christ.

the MEANS of

Therefore go and make disciples of all nations, baptizing them in the name of the Father and of the Son and of the Holy Spirit.

Matthew 28:19

The Lord Jesus breathed on His disciples and said, "Receive the Holy Spirit. If you forgive anyone his sins, they are forgiven; if you do not forgive them, they are not forgiven."

John 20:22–23

Our Lord Jesus Christ, on the night when He was betrayed, took bread, and when He had given thanks, He broke it and gave it to the disciples and said: "Take, eat; this is My body, which is given for you. This do in remembrance of Me." In the same way also He took the cup after supper, and when He had given thanks, He gave it to them, saying, "Drink of it, all of you; this cup is the new testament in My blood, which is shed for you for the forgiveness of sins. This do, as often as you drink it, in remembrance of Me."

Matthew 26:26–28;
Mark 14:22–24;
Luke 22:19–20;
1 Corinthians 11:23–25

GRACE

Water

Forgiveness

Word

Cup

Bread

In the 1700s, numerous doctors proposed the "water cure" for every ~~aliment~~ ailment known to humanity. The "water cure" sometimes denoted simple daily bathing. But sometimes it included a special trip to a particular spring or the guzzling of outrageous quantities of natural mineral water. By 1900, the water cure fad had ended. But, thankfully, it left behind the one feature of the movement with enduring health benefits: daily washing with soap and water.

In the water and words of Baptism, God offers us a profound and powerful cure. Just as simple soap and water combine to create a powerful defense against disease, the water and the Word of Baptism combine for our spiritual benefit and defense.[Tu]

Humble Washing

As pictured here, Baptism has the humblest character. The minister pours, sprinkles, or immerses someone with water, adding these simple words from Jesus: "In the name of the Father and of the Son and of the Holy Spirit." The whole act may seem like child's play.[W]

But don't let the simplicity of Baptism deceive you! God has promised the most profound blessings through these humble means. For example, the prophet Ezekiel foretold the blessings of Baptism and its power to change the heart.[Th] Like soap combining with water to cleanse the body, the cleansing Word of God combines with the water of Baptism. Baptism provides more than a washing of the body. It cleanses hearts from the guilt and stain of sin.

Follow Jesus

At the beginning of His earthly ministry, Jesus Himself was baptized in the Jordan River. As the Son of God, Jesus did not need the washing of Baptism. He already had perfect righteousness. But He explained to John that He sought Baptism "to fulfill all righteousness."[F] In this way, Jesus prepared Baptism for you and all who would follow Him.[S]

If you have been baptized, then rejoice in the washing that God has given you by water and the Word. Remember and celebrate your Baptism by returning to the words of your Baptism each day: in the name of the Father and of the Son and of the Holy Spirit.

Emma Brownlow (1832–1905). *The Christening.*

Baptism

What is Baptism?

Baptism is not just plain water, but it is the water included in God's command and combined with God's word.

Meditations: Change Blessing Praise Request

M Read the article on page 84. Tu Ephesians 5:25–30. What results from the washing that God provides in Baptism?
W Luke 18:9–17. Reflect on the tapestry on the back wall in the painting.
Th Ezekiel 36:24–32. How does Baptism transform the heart? F Matthew 3:4–17. Why did people come to John for Baptism?
S Hebrews 10:15–25. What gives Baptism its power?

Which is that word of God?

Christ our Lord says in the last chapter of Matthew: "Therefore go and make disciples of all nations, baptizing them in the name of the Father and of the Son and of the Holy Spirit." [Matthew 28:19]

What benefits does Baptism give?

It works forgiveness of sins, rescues from death and the devil, and gives eternal salvation to all who believe this, as the words and promises of God declare.

Which are these words and promises of God?

Christ our Lord says in the last chapter of Mark: "Whoever believes and is baptized will be saved, but whoever does not believe will be condemned." [Mark 16:16]

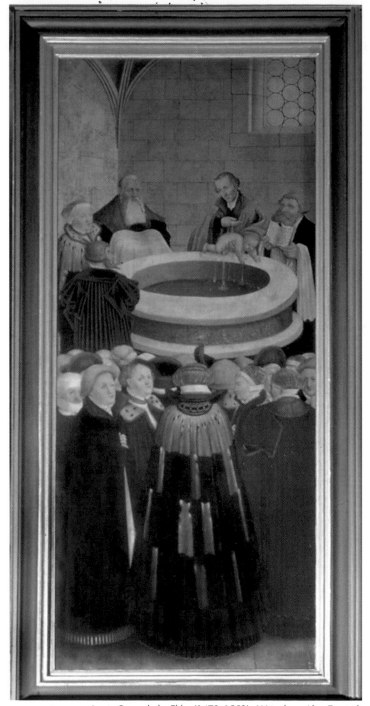

Lucas Cranach the Elder (1472–1553). *Wittenberg Altar Tryptych.*

Meditations: Change Blessing Praise Request
MRead the article on page 87. TuMatthew 28:16–20. Where is Jesus according to this passage?
WRomans 3:9–20. Summarize the effects of sin. ThJohn 3:1–8. How does Jesus describe the work of the Spirit?
FActs 2:36–41. Whom does God call through Baptism? SGalatians 3:22–29. Reflect on how Baptism transforms the church.

Cut pp. 23-24

In Cranach's famous altar painting at the parish church of Wittenberg, the congregation gathers to witness the Baptism of a small child in the church's large font. Officiating is Philip Melancthon. To Philip's right stands the baby's godfather, none other than the painter himself, Lucas Cranach, his arms ready to receive the infant fresh from its baptismal washing.

The water pouring off the child is ordinary water. But not just plain water. It is water included in God's command and combined with God's own Word: "Therefore go and make disciples of all nations, baptizing them in the name of the Father and of the Son and of the Holy Spirit."[Tu] In other words, God Himself provides the power of Baptism. There, God Himself washes away sin, destroys death, delivers from the devil's tyranny, and bestows everlasting life for everyone who believes.

For Everyone

Jesus commanded Baptism for everyone. He never restricted Baptism by race, age, size, or gender. Our gracious God is nondiscriminatory and all-inclusive in both His command and promise: "all nations" must be baptized because "all nations" have fallen under the curse of sin and death.[W] Yet, at the same time, "all nations" have been redeemed by the blood of God's own Son. Therefore, there are no exceptions or exclusions. "All nations" must hear and receive this Gospel for their souls' salvation.[Th]

Who would exclude from Baptism anyone whom God has included in His salvation (Mark 10:13–15)? Every single person—whether adult or infant, mentally advanced or handicapped—falls under the curse of sin. Yet God includes each and every person in His gracious rescue plan to save all humanity from sin and death.[F]

All through Christ

Each time you see an adult or infant being baptized, you witness God's gracious plan in action. Holy Baptism is a bath of regeneration, a washing of rebirth and renewal by the Holy Spirit that offers, gives, and seals the life of Christ to sinners who believe in Him. In this water Jesus gives His very life to rescue souls from sin, death, and hell.

What joy to know that the promise excludes no one—not even you! Baptized into Christ, you too may claim a place within God's kingdom by His grace.[S]

It came by water. A ship carrying Englishmen appeared off North America in 1607. The ship brought not just new people but a new way of life.

Friendly Pocahantas, daughter of a Powhantan Indian chief, frequently visited these newcomers. At 18, Pocahontas became a Christian. Through the waters of Holy Baptism, she joined the family of all who receive the forgiveness and eternal life that Jesus earned for all nations.[Tu] Just as water brought newcomers and a new way of life to the land of Pocahantas, the water and Word of Baptism brought Pocahantas to a new and eternal life.[W]

Living a New Life

At her Baptism, Pocahantas took the biblical name "Rebecca" to mark the beginning of her new life. She married a settler named John Rolfe and gave birth to a son. Rebecca's new life carried her far from the land of her birth.[Th] Her family traveled to England, where she attracted great attention as an American princess in the court of King James I and in the best of English society.

Like Pocahantas, all people baptized into Christ can anticipate a new life, knowing that the Holy Spirit will encourage and equip them with His life-giving Word.[F] Each day as you leave the past behind, you can find strength, direction, and hope in God's Word. You can face all of life's uncertainties and adventures, confident that, like Pocahantas, you are an heir of eternal life through your Baptism into Christ.[S]

> All who believe and are baptized Shall see the Lord's salvation;
> Baptized into the death of Christ, They are a new creation;
> Through Christ's redemption they will stand
> Among the glorious heav'nly band Of ev'ry tribe and nation.
>
> With one accord, O God, we pray, Grant us Your Holy Spirit;
> Help us in our infirmity Through Jesus' blood and merit;
> Grant us to grow in grace each day
> By holy Baptism that we may Eternal life inherit.
>
> Thomas H. Kingo; tr. George A. T. Rygh

John Gadsby Chapman (1808–1889). *Baptism of Pocahontas.*

How can water do such great things?

Certainly not just water, but the word of God in and with the water does these things, along with the faith which trusts this word of God in the water. For without God's word the water is plain water and no Baptism. But with the word of God it is a Baptism, that is, a life-giving water, rich in grace, and a washing of the new birth in the Holy Spirit, as St. Paul says in Titus, chapter three: "He saved us through the washing of rebirth and renewal by the Holy Spirit, whom He poured out on us generously through Jesus Christ our Savior, so that, having been justified by His grace, we might become heirs having the hope of eternal life. This is a trustworthy saying." [Titus 3:5–8]

Meditations: Change Blessing Praise Request

Mead the article on page 88. TuActs 16:6–15. How does the woman in this passage become a Christian? W1 Peter 3:18–4:2. How does Baptism save? ThGenesis 24:52–67. Reflect on how God guided the life of Pocahontas and the biblical Rebekah. FJohn 5:24–40. When does eternal life begin for you? STitus 3:3–8. Reflect on your inheritance as a Christian.

*What does such baptizing
with water indicate?*

It indicates that the Old Adam in
us should by daily contrition and
repentance be drowned and die
with all sins and evil desires,
and that a new man should daily
emerge and arise to live before
God in righteousness and purity
forever.

Where is this written?

St. Paul writes in Romans
chapter six: "We were therefore
buried with Him through baptism
into death in order that, just as
Christ was raised from the dead
through the glory of the Father,
we too may live a new life."
[Romans 6:4]

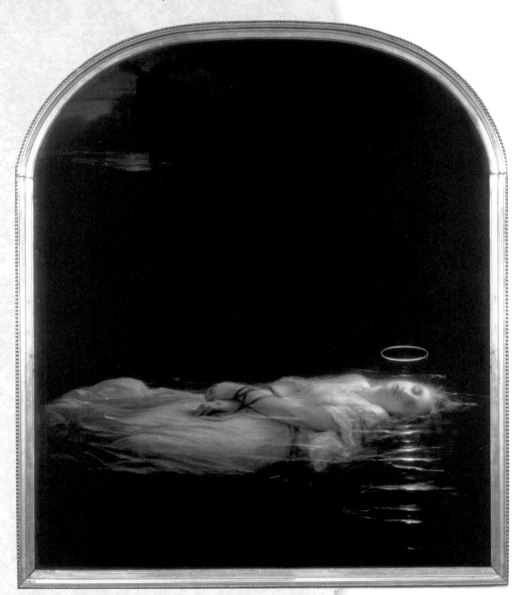

Hippolyte-Paul Delaroche (1797–1856). *The Young Martyr.*

Meditations: Change Blessing Praise Request
MRead the article on page 91. TuMark 10:35–45. What "baptism" does Jesus have in view in this passage? (Note verse 45.)
WRomans 6:1–10. Why is our death in Baptism necessary?
ThRomans 5:12–19. Reflect on the pattern made by Adam and the pattern made by Christ.
FEphesians 4:4–16. What unites all true Christians? SColossians 2:6–15. What is the state of the sinful nature?

Alongside the Baptism commanded by Jesus, the early Christians talked about another baptism: the baptism by blood. Baptism by blood referred to the death from persecution that many early Christians suffered during the first three centuries after Christ.[Tu] Like the young woman pictured here, bound hand and foot and thrown into the Tiber River by the Romans, thousands of early Christians affirmed their faith by suffering persecution and death.

The apostle Paul makes a similar connection between Baptism, death, and life. As he explains in Romans 6, Baptism buries us with Christ so that we might rise again and live a new life through faith in His blood.[W]

Buried with Christ

Baptism works like death because in Baptism the Lord puts to death our sinful nature, the "Old Adam."[Th] Though Baptism is a one-time event,[F] we need to return to the promise of our Baptism daily. That's because our sinful nature constantly "bobs" to the surface. It refuses to stay buried!

Each time we confess our sins and ask for forgiveness through the death and resurrection of Christ, God renews in us the blessings of our Baptism. He buries us with Christ and raises us renewed.

Raised to New Life

When the dark flood of persecution, hardship, or temptation threatens you, don't struggle to overcome it in your own power. Trust in the precious blood of Jesus and the Baptism you received in His name. Through daily contrition and repentance, He will bear you up. He will rescue you and give you new life![S]

martyreo — to witness (as in talking about the thing you believe in)

Righteousness

Cut pp. 26

I n this dark painting, Lorenzo Lotto captures the sorrowful mood of his friend Gregoro Belo. Gregoro has discovered a compelling passage in a book of sermons by Gregory the Great. The words convict him. As a gesture of his anguish over sin, Gregoro balls his fist and strikes his breast.

Like Gregoro, you too feel anguish over sin. At times, your conscience assaults you and God's Law reminds you of your failures. But as you meditate on God's commandments and confess your faults, do not let dark moods overwhelm you. Do not seek to pay for your sins by punishing yourself.[Tu] Instead, seek the counsel of your pastor or of a faithful Christian friend.

Confess Your Sins

The apostle James writes, "Confess your sins to each other and pray for each other so that you may be healed."[W] At first the idea of admitting your weaknesses and mistakes may seem crazy. You may cringe at the idea of dropping your defenses. The moment before you make confession, you may fear that someone will use your confession against you. After all, that's the way the world works—by blackmail and abuse.

But before you withdraw, take note of the second part of the apostle's counsel, "so that you may be healed." When people hold in their sins, fears, and anxieties, they pay a horrible price. Unconfessed sin gnaws at the soul the way unseen worms gnaw at fruit. Outwardly, a person may appear whole. Inwardly, many are hollow. They need healing.[Th]

Healing through Christ

Thanks be to God. He provides for your healing. Take note of the scene in the upper left corner of the painting. This inset depicts the meditation of Gregoro's heart. Though he has struck his breast in a gesture of confession, he also remembers the source of his healing.[F]

Jesus Christ, who hung on the cross for the forgiveness of sins, provided for Gregoro's forgiveness and yours. When you confess your sins to a pastor or a fellow Christian and hear from that person God's promise of forgiveness, you've heard from heaven itself! After His death and resurrection Jesus sent His apostles specifically for this purpose: to comfort troubled souls and heal broken hearts. Don't punish yourself by holding onto your sins.[S] Confide in a called servant of the Gospel and receive the comfort that only the Gospel can give.

What is Confession?

Confession has two parts. First, that we confess our sins, and second, that we receive absolution, that is, forgiveness, from the pastor as from God Himself, not doubting, but firmly believing that by it our sins are forgiven before God in heaven.

Lorenzo Lotto (c.1480–1556). *Brother Gregoro Belo of Vicenza.*

Meditations: Change Blessing Praise Request

MRead the article on page 92. TuIsaiah 53:1–12. Reflect on how Jesus already bore your punishment.
WJames 5:13–20. What might encourage or discourage you from confessing your sins to another person?
ThLuke 4:14–21. What did Jesus come to do? FLuke 23:20–34. Reflect on Jesus' prayer.
SPsalm 32:1–7. How did the psalmist find relief?

What sins should we confess?

Before God we should plead guilty of all sins, even those we are not aware of, as we do in the Lord's Prayer; but before the pastor we should confess only those sins which we know and feel in our hearts.

Which are these?

Consider your place in life according to the Ten Commandments: Are you a father, mother, son, daughter, husband, wife, or worker? Have you been disobedient, unfaithful, or lazy? Have you been hot-tempered, rude, or quarrelsome? Have you hurt someone by your words or deeds? Have you stolen, been negligent, wasted anything, or done any harm?

Georges de la Tour (1593–1652). *The Penitent Magdalen.*

Meditations: Change Blessing Praise Request

MRead the article on page 95. TuLuke 7:36–8:3. The woman in Luke 7 probably isn't Mary. But what fact about Mary does 8:2 reveal?

WJames 1:19–27. What mirror does James have in view? How does it work in your life?

ThEzekiel 16:9–19. How did Israel ruin its garments? FMatthew 19:16–26. Answer the disciples' question in verse 25.

S1 John 1:8–2:2. How does God demonstrate His faithfulness to you?

Mary Magdalene strikes a familiar pose. Sitting before her mirror, she examines herself like any young woman. However, the trinkets of Mary's former trade lie discarded on the table and floor. According to tradition, Mary lived as a prostitute.[Tu] In the painting she takes an honest look at her cheap and empty life and calls it by name: death. In her lap she holds a skull, the symbol of the sure and certain penalty for sin.

Sin causes addiction. That's us—compulsive sinners. Locked in the familiar cycle of sin, remorse, guilt, and more sin, there seems to be no way out of sin's slavery. Apart from Christ, that is. He alone breaks the bonds of sin and sets prisoners free.

The Mirror

This freedom all begins when by faith sinners take an honest look at their place in life in God's mirror, the Ten Commandments.[W] There, what we had assumed to be the bright garments of our achievements are shown for what they really are: tattered and torn, ragged with sin and death.[Th] We learn the art of self-examination so that we may confess our sin and be rid of it.

Two points of reference are essential: the Ten Commandments and our place in life. Some of us are fathers, some mothers, all of us are sons or daughters. We could be husbands, wives, or workers. In whatever position we find ourselves in home or society, we may be sure that God has placed us there, with unique roles and responsibilities. God intends to use every Christian as His instrument, providing for the needs of all creation through the deeds of love He gives us all to do in daily life.[F]

Peace through Christ

When we look at our lives in the unflinching light of God's holy Law, we see our sin and we know what to confess before the throne of God. There we find courage to admit our guilt and shame: "God, have mercy on me, a sinner" (Luke 18:13).

To deny our sin is to call God a liar. But when we confess our sins, He is faithful and just to forgive our sins and cleanse us from all unrighteousness in Jesus' name.[S]

He is faithful and just

Keys not only lock and unlock our homes. They also open and close prison cells. They secure or unleash nuclear warheads. Keys represent the authority or stewardship of those who hold them.[Tu]

When Jesus gave the "keys of the kingdom of heaven" to His disciples, He gave them remarkable authority. The keys mentioned by Jesus were not literal keys, like those in the painting here. The keys represent the authority Christ gave His church to lock or unlock heaven through the means of grace.

Keys of Heaven

Jesus first mentions the keys of the kingdom of heaven in Matthew 16.[W] He told His followers that these keys would lock or unlock heaven. During Jesus' ministry, He transferred this authority to His disciples from the priests, scribes, and Pharisees.[Th] These leaders had misused the gifts of God, shutting people out of heaven and denying them the assurance of the mercy He wanted them to have.

Before going to the cross, Jesus explained to the disciples how and when they should use these keys. When people refuse to repent, the disciples should "bind" people in their sins. They should use the condemning power of God's Law, which shows people their sins and locks heaven against them if they do not repent. God's church holds this powerful key.

However, God does not want to lock heaven against anyone. He wants all people to receive His forgiveness and enter heaven. Therefore, Jesus urged His disciples to "loose" all repentant people from their sins through the means of grace: Baptism, the preaching of the Gospel (absolution), and the Lord's Supper. Because these means bestow God's grace or favor, they open heaven for everyone who receives them in faith.[F]

Blessings of Heaven

Rejoice in how God graciously provides for your salvation and the salvation of the whole world. Do not hold onto your sin, which holds you down and shuts heaven against you. Gladly hear the preaching of God's Word. Support the called servants of the Gospel who use these keys publicly on the Lord's behalf for building up His church.[S]

When you witness a Baptism, hear the Gospel preached, or partake of the Lord's Supper, do not imagine that you partake of mere ceremonies. Through these means of grace, held by God's church, God opens to you all the blessings of heaven. These means of grace are not mere symbols. They exercise God's authority on earth for your benefit.

God's authority on earth

Nicolas Poussin (1594–1665). *The Sacrament of Ordination.*

What is the Office of the Keys?

The Office of the Keys is that special authority which Christ has given to His church on earth to forgive the sins of repentant sinners, but to withhold forgiveness from the unrepentant as long as they do not repent.

Where is this written?

This is what St. John the Evangelist writes in chapter twenty: The Lord Jesus breathed on His disciples and said, "Receive the Holy Spirit. If you forgive anyone his sins, they are forgiven; if you do not forgive them, they are not forgiven." [John 20:22–23]

Meditations: Change Blessing Praise Request
MRead the article on page 96.
TuIsaiah 22:15–24. How do the examples of Shebna and Eliakim help you understand the Office of the Keys?
WMatthew 16:13–20. On what will Christ build the church? ThMatthew 23:1–13. How did the scribes and Pharisees misuse the keys?
FMatthew 18:12–20. How should the keys work in your life? SJohn 20:19–23. What comfort does this passage offer to you?

dev.7

What do you believe according to these words?

I believe that when the called ministers of Christ deal with us by His divine command, in particular when they exclude openly unrepentant sinners from the Christian congregation and absolve those who repent of their sins and want to do better, this is just as valid and certain, even in heaven, as if Christ our dear Lord dealt with us Himself.

Florentine School. *Antonio Hurling Dung.* 1502.

Meditations: Change Blessing Praise Request

M Read the article on page 99.

Tu 2 Corinthians 2:1–11. Reflect on how the apostle Paul leads and supports the congregation in forgiveness.

W 1 Timothy 3. What has God entrusted to public ministers? Th Jeremiah 1:4–10. How did God change Jeremiah at his calling?

F Isaiah 6:1–8. How does Isaiah respond to the personal absolution that God gave him?

S Matthew 10:32–42. Describe the relationship between the Lord and His servants.

In His merciful love, Jesus Christ has not only ransomed us from sin by His death, but He has also provided for the continual forgiveness of sins in His church. He has commissioned His church to continue His work on earth by forgiving the sins of penitent sinners in His name and stead. His called servants exercise this power publicly for the church.[Tu]

Full Forgiveness

That's the way it works still today in Christ's church. Whenever the called ministers of Christ deal with us by His divine command, they do His heavenly work here on earth.[W] Sins are erased, hearts are cleansed, and souls are restored in Jesus' name. By the grace of God, our pastor's absolution is valid and certain not merely on earth, but also in heaven—as if Christ, our dear Lord, dealt with us Himself!

When sin has its way with us, all too often we feel so defiled and dirty that there seems no way on earth we could ever be forgiven. At these times, we need to seek out our pastor, who will deal with us compassionately and gently in Jesus' name. We can confess openly, without fear, for every pastor is under solemn obligation never to divulge sins spoken to him in confession. We should think of his ears as God's ears and freely give voice to the hurt and burden of our sin. More than that, we should regard our pastor's mouth as God's mouth[Th] when the pastor speaks God's own absolving Word that our heart is aching to hear.

Valid and Certain

As the example of Antonio shows, sin happens. Ever since Adam and Eve first rebelled against God, the sinful mind is hostile toward God, constantly hatching plots that defy Him and injure our neighbor. The problem goes still deeper: the human heart itself is the culprit. Even the most moral and upright person has a heart inwardly polluted by sin and filth, the continual source of all kinds of mischief that wars against the soul (Matthew 15:19).

Yet imagine that you had a direct line to heaven and were able to hear God's own voice with a personalized word of forgiveness tailor-made just for you.[F] Wouldn't that be a terrific, freeing experience? That's exactly what Jesus Christ has provided for His church in the gift of absolution through the mouth of His called servants. That Word erases sin, drives out both fear and shame, and in its place bestows the very life of Christ to all who love and trust in Him. Wouldn't you like to hear that Word for yourself?[S]

In this medieval painting, the artist portrays the foolishness of human sin in action. In 1501 Antonio di Giuseppe Rinaldeschi vandalized an image of Jesus' mother by throwing dung on it. Apparently, Antonio had just lost a bet and blamed God for his failure. Enraged, he threw the dung and fled the city. For this sacrilege a mob arrested and condemned him. Yet another panel of the painting shows the penitent Antonio receiving absolution for all his sins, including the sins the mob considered unforgivable.

E ach year wars and disasters uproot millions of families. However, as these desperate families flock together, bullets and violent weather do not present the greatest threats. Simple thirst and hunger present the greatest disaster threat to refugees.

According to the Bible, the Christian life through this world is one of pilgrimage. Like refugees, Christians travel amidst the troubles of life on their way to a more permanent homeland. As pictured here, our Lord provides for our needs on our spiritual journey through a special meal: Christ's body and blood given and shed to sustain your life.[Tu]

Hunger and Thirst

Hunger and thirst are the most basic human urges. In the Lord's Supper, Jesus satisfies those most basic urges in a unique way. Whereas other meals offer benefits that last for the moment, the Lord's Supper offers an eternal benefit for those who eat and drink in faith. Through His body and blood in the Lord's Supper, Jesus promises us the forgiveness of sins and a foretaste of the eternal feast with Him in heaven.[W]

Some have questioned Jesus' promise, wondering, "How can He give us His body and blood to eat and drink? Surely His words are symbolic." However, the earliest Christians—the first wave of refugees to flee this sin-starved world—did not take Jesus' words as mere symbolism. For example, the apostle Paul affirmed Jesus' promise in the Lord's Supper. He noted that the cup and the bread are a participation (communing, sharing) in the actual body and blood of Jesus.[Th] Jesus would not give His weary disciples symbolic gestures when they need real food![F]

Real Food

Just as hungry refugees need more than faint promises or mere hope that things will be better someday, God's people need something more. Jesus meets the genuine needs of His people by sustaining them with His very life's blood. Each time you receive the Lord's Supper in faith, you receive a life-giving transfusion. The body and blood of Christ mingle with your body and blood in a miracle surpassing all the other wonders of heaven and earth.

Don't grow faint in your faith. Don't collapse from spiritual starvation. Draw near and take part in Christ's Holy Supper. He will sustain you and satisfy your needs of body and soul.[S]

True body and blood

Altar Frontal from Torslunde Church. 1561.

What is the Sacrament of the Altar?

It is the true body and blood of our Lord Jesus Christ under the bread and wine, instituted by Christ Himself for us Christians to eat and to drink.

Meditations: Change Blessing Praise Request

M Read the article on page 100. Tu Psalm 34:1–10. Reflect on the offer in verse 8.
W Matthew 26:17–30. What do you meditate on during the Lord's Supper?
Th 1 Corinthians 10:14–21. Why did Jesus use one loaf and one cup? F John 6:52–59. Reflect on the question from the crowd in verse 52.
S Isaiah 55:1–11. What accomplishes God's purpose for you?

Salvador Dali (1904–1989). *The Last Supper.*

Where is this written?

The holy Evangelists Matthew, Mark, Luke, and St. Paul write: Our Lord Jesus Christ, on the night when He was betrayed, took bread, and when He had given thanks, He broke it and gave it to the disciples and said: "Take, eat; this is My body, which is given for you. This do in remembrance of Me."

In the same way also He took the cup after supper, and when He had given thanks, He gave it to them, saying, "Drink of it, all of you; this cup is the new testament in My blood, which is shed for you for the forgiveness of sins. This do, as often as you drink it, in remembrance of Me."

Meditations: Change Blessing Praise Request
^MRead the article on page 103. ^{Tu}Luke 22:13–30. What do verses 16 and 18 tell you about Jesus and the Lord's Supper?
^W1 Corinthians 11:17–26. How does the Lord's Supper serve as proclamation?
ThJohn 6:41–51. Do you find Jesus' words offensive? Why or why not?
^FExodus 12:1–14. How is Passover like the Lord's Supper? ^SActs 2:42–47. Reflect on the fellowship of the first Christians.

After years of estrangement from the church, Salvador Dali expressed his renewed faith in this painting and in several others with religious themes. Dali shows the table of the Upper Room transformed into an altar, while vested disciples bow their heads in reverence at the great mystery unfolded in the Holy Supper. Earthly bread and wine stand ready on the table, while Christ points to His body, which He will lay down in death for the sins of the world. His victory over death is seen in the risen torso suspended above.[Tu]

At the Lord's Table, as often as we eat that bread and drink that cup, we proclaim the Lord's death until He comes again in glory.[W] But this meal is no mere symbol. The bread we break and the cup we bless are an actual participation in the body and blood once given and shed for the forgiveness of sins.

One Sacrifice

In the Supper, the Lord Jesus feeds His church with His very body and true blood. The same flesh and blood that hung upon His cross at Calvary, rose from the dead, and ascended into heaven is here provided in earthly bread and wine for us Christians to eat and drink. We need not ascend into heaven to come into contact with God. In this holy sacrament the exalted heavenly Christ comes down to earth so that we may feed on Him not just in faith, but by mouth as well.[Th]

As Israel once ate from the very sacrifice that cleansed them from sin, in this sacrament Jesus invites His church to feed on His atoning sacrifice.[F] It is His continuing testament to His church, a sign and seal of the forgiveness He earned once and for all when He gave His life at the cross. Here we have tangible encouragement for faith. We already know that all the sins of all the world have been taken away by the death and resurrection of Jesus, but here that forgiveness is personalized. *"Take, eat; this is My body, which is given for you." "This cup is the new testament in My blood, which is shed for you for the forgiveness of sins."* As the living Father sent Christ and Christ lives because of the Father, so all who feed on Christ will live because of Christ.[S]

He is the living bread from heaven, come down to bring life to the world. Whoever eats His flesh and drinks His blood will live forever, for whoever believes in Christ has life everlasting. Thus, until He comes again, we continually eat and drink His flesh and blood, living always by faith in Jesus' name!

I n 1419, after seeing Jan Hus and Jerome of Prague burned at the stake, the people of Bohemia rebelled against church authorities and local rulers. At the heart of this dispute was a simple practice, one that many Christians take for granted today: drinking from the cup during the Lord's Supper. In 1281 a medieval church law had ordered that only the clergy could drink from the cup. But a century later, after studying God's Word, the Bohemians sought to have the cup restored to them.[Tu]

Believe the Word

God's Word teaches us how we should receive the Lord's Supper and what benefits we receive in this sacrament.[W] The Lord's Supper is more than a memorial meal, a ceremony, or a custom subject to man-made rules or opinions.

Jesus tells us the main benefit of the Lord's Supper when He says that His blood was "shed for you for the forgiveness of sins." Through the humble means of bread and wine, we receive the very life of Christ Himself.[Th] Who would toy with these words or the way in which Jesus gives us these benefits?

Hunger and Thirst

Look into the eyes of the Bohemian preacher. Take note of the people gathered around him. They left the comfortable walls of their churches and homes behind, hungering and thirsting for the privilege of eating the body and drinking the blood of Christ according to Jesus' own words of promise.[F]

The next time your congregation offers the Lord's Supper, humbly prepare for the Sacrament.[S] Confess your sins. Hunger for Christ's body. Thirst for the cup. Believe His promise that He gives His body and blood for the forgiveness of all your sins. Jesus will give you exactly what His words promise: forgiveness, life, and salvation.

Carl Friedrich Lessing (1808–1880). *Hussite Sermon.*

What is the benefit of this eating and drinking?

These words, "Given and shed for you for the forgiveness of sins," show us that in the Sacrament forgiveness of sins, life, and salvation are given us through these words. For where there is forgiveness of sins, there is also life and salvation.

How can bodily eating and drinking do such great things?

Certainly not just eating and drinking do these things, but the words written here: "Given and shed for you for the forgiveness of sins." These words, along with the bodily eating and drinking, are the main thing in the Sacrament. Whoever believes these words has exactly what they say: "forgiveness of sins."

Meditations: Change Blessing Praise Request
MRead the article on page 104. TuMark 7:5–15. Why were these traditions wrong?
WMark 14:13–26. What does Jesus promise you in this passage? ThJohn 6:25–35. What is the "bread of God"?
FPsalm 42:1–11. Answer the question in verse 10. SPsalm 116:7–19. What thanks would you offer to the Lord?

Who receives this sacrament worthily?

Fasting and bodily preparation are certainly fine outward training. But that person is truly worthy and well prepared who has faith in these words: "Given and shed for you for the forgiveness of sins." But anyone who does not believe these words or doubts them is unworthy and unprepared, for the words "for you" require all hearts to believe.

David Alfaro Siqueiros (1896–1974). *The Sob.* 1939.

Meditations: Change Blessing Praise Request
MRead the article on page 107. TuJohn 14:1–13. What makes Jesus trustworthy?
WRomans 5:6–11. How does verse 6 describe your life? Th1 Corinthians 11:23–32. Why is preparing for the Lord's Supper important?
FRevelation 3:14–22. According to verse 19, why repent? SIsaiah 65:17–25. What part of this passage encourages you the most?

Your eyes hold about 16 milliliters of tears. When your eyes feel irritated or moistened with grief, they will shed more tears. But there's a limit to tears. Though they have a cleansing effect and will often make you feel better, the tears you shed can never wash away your pain or prepare you for what's to come.

When you prepare for the Lord's Supper, the shedding of tears in sorrow, the disciplining of the body through fasting, and the announcement of your intention to go to the Sacrament are all excellent steps. But the Lord's Supper requires something more, something beyond tears or any other bodily preparation. By the shedding of His blood, the Lord calls you to *trust* in Him for the forgiveness of all your sins.[Tu]

Trust in the Blood

When the pains of life or your sorrow over sin casts you into the dust, remember that you do not need to bear these pains or sorrows in your own strength. Christ bore these pains and sorrows for you when He shed His blood for the forgiveness of your sins and the salvation of your soul.

Christ does not ask you to follow Him by your own power of commitment or demonstration of sincerity.[W] The Lord's Supper is not an exercise God requires by which you make yourself worthy of Christ. You are not worthy of Him, and even gallons of tears cannot make you worthy! Instead, Jesus bids you to trust Him, to confess Him as the one worthy sacrifice for all your sins. Your preparation for His Supper begins in Him, in His tears and His blood.[Th]

Tears of Joy

The Book of Revelation contains a series of letters through which Jesus calls congregations to repent and remain steadfast. In the last letter, Jesus urges the people to hear His voice and join with Him in a meal of consolation.[F] That's what Christ calls you to do in the Lord's Supper: repent and trust in Him.

Each time you prepare for the Lord's Supper, hear the voice of Jesus calling you away from your sins. Hear His promise to abide with you and care for you. Though you shed a thousand tears in sorrow, He will dry your eyes. Though your eyes fail for tears, His forgiving voice will fill your heart with faith and your eyes with tears of joy.[S]

Holy Orders

Your Gifts

Bless Us

DAILY

DEVOTION

In the name . . .

I thank You, my heavenly Father . . .

The eyes of all look to You . . .

Our Father . . .

Bless us and these Your gifts . . .

Give thanks to the Lord, for He is good . . .

We thank You . . .

Holy Orders

How the head of the family should teach his household
to pray morning and evening

In the morning when you get up or in the evening when you go to bed, make the sign of the holy cross and say:

In the name of the Father and of the Son and of the Holy Spirit. Amen.

Then, kneeling or standing, repeat the Creed and the Lord's Prayer. If you choose, you may also say this little prayer:

I thank You, my heavenly Father, through Jesus Christ, Your dear Son,

MORNING PRAYER

that You have kept me this night
from all harm and danger;
and I pray that You would
keep me this day also from sin
and every evil,
that all my doings and life
may please You.

EVENING PRAYER

that You have graciously
kept me this day; and I pray
that You would forgive me
all my sins where I have
done wrong, and graciously
keep me this night.

For into Your hands I commend myself, my body and soul, and all things. Let Your holy angel be with me, that the evil foe may have no power over me. Amen.

Then go joyfully to your work,
singing a hymn, like that
of the Ten Commandments,
or whatever your devotion
may suggest.

Then go to sleep at once and
in good cheer.

Meditations: Change Blessing Praise Request
[M]Read the article on page 111. [Tu]Psalm 113. Answer the question in verses 5 and 6. [W]Psalm 136. Why thank Him?
[Th]Psalm 25:1–11. Compare the personal nature of this prayer to your prayers.
[F]Psalm 10:12–17. Whom might you intercede for today? [S]Psalm 146. Whom does the psalmist address? (See verse 1.)

Henry Le Jeune (1819–1904). *A Prayer.*

Wonder dances before a child's eyes. Prayer seems wonderful: the opportunity to bring requests to someone with unlimited power. But what to ask? What to leave out? What do you say to someone who knows you from the moment you get up to the moment you lie down again?[Tu]

The words of our prayers often hang on the moment of need. But a model, an outline, a place to start is a wonderful help. The prayers on the opposite page serve as models of Christian devotion. Commit them to heart. Use them morning and evening to grow in your understanding of prayer as thanksgiving,[W] request,[Th] intercession,[F] and praise.[S] Your dear Father in heaven anxiously awaits your requests and will answer them through His dear Son, Jesus Christ.

Henry Ossawa Tanner (1859–1937). *The Thankful Poor.*

W hen Dr. Martin Luther died, his mourners discovered in his pocket a scrap of paper with one sentence written on it. This sentence is perhaps Luther's greatest writing of all: "We are beggars—that is true." These words summarize the entire Christian life. Everything we have comes from God.[Tu]

Good Gifts from God

Maybe you neglect prayer, even your table prayers. Or perhaps you automatically repeat a prayer you learned as a child without even thinking about God or His gifts. If so, spend a few moments meditating on Luther's words "We are beggars—that is true." Whether you live in abundance or as humbly as the people in this painting,[W] take inventory of your life and realize anew the countless gifts that God has given to you! In addition to the most precious gift of salvation through Jesus, your merciful Father abundantly pours out for you everything you need to support your body and life.[Th]

God provides daily bread to everyone, even those who hate Him. Many receive these gifts without recognizing His provision or thanking Him for it. Receive your daily bread differently. Thank God for all you have and live contentedly with it.[F] Even more so, let your daily bread remind you of the greater gifts that God has given to you: forgiveness of sins, life, and salvation through His Son.[S]

How the head of the family should teach his household to ask a blessing and return thanks

ASKING A BLESSING

The children and members of the household shall go to the table reverently, fold their hands, and say:

The eyes of all look to You, O Lord, and You give them their food at the proper time. You open Your hand and satisfy the desires of every living thing. [Psalm 145:15–16]

Then shall be said the Lord's Prayer and the following:

Lord God, heavenly Father, bless us and these Your gifts which we receive from Your bountiful goodness, through Jesus Christ, our Lord. Amen.

RETURNING THANKS

Also, after eating, they shall, in like manner, reverently and with folded hands say:

Give thanks to the Lord, for He is good. His love endures forever. He gives food to every creature. He provides food for the cattle and for the young ravens when they call. His pleasure is not in the strength of the horse, nor His delight in the legs of a man; the Lord delights in those who fear Him, who put their hope in His unfailing love. [Psalm 136:1, 25; 147:9–11]

Then shall be said the Lord's Prayer and the following:

We thank You, Lord God, heavenly Father, for all Your benefits, through Jesus Christ, our Lord, who lives and reigns with You and the Holy Spirit forever and ever. Amen.

Meditations: Change Blessing Praise Request
[M]Read the article on page 112. [Tu]Psalm 145:13–21. Reflect on God's timing. [W]Philippians 4:4–13. How do you present your requests? [Th]Matthew 6:25–34. What does Jesus promise in this passage? [F]1 Timothy 6:6–16. What contentment does Christ offer? [S]2 Corinthians 4:16–5:5. Why did God make you?

Table of Duties

Certain passages of Scripture for various holy orders and positions, admonishing them about their duties and responsibilities

p35

TO BISHOPS, PASTORS, AND PREACHERS

The overseer must be above reproach, the husband of but one wife, temperate, self-controlled, respectable, hospitable, able to teach, not given to drunkenness, not violent but gentle, not quarrelsome, not a lover of money. He must manage his own family well and see that his children obey him with proper respect. 1 Timothy 3:2–4

He must not be a recent convert, or he may become conceited and fall under the same judgment as the devil. 1 Timothy 3:6

He must hold firmly to the trustworthy message as it has been taught, so that he can encourage others by sound doctrine and refute those who oppose it. Titus 1:9

p36

WHAT THE HEARERS OWE THEIR PASTORS

The Lord has commanded that those who preach the gospel should receive their living from the gospel. 1 Corinthians 9:14

Anyone who receives instruction in the word must share all good things with his instructor. Do not be deceived: God cannot be mocked. A man reaps what he sows. Galatians 6:6–7

The elders who direct the affairs of the church well are worthy of double honor, especially those whose work is preaching and teaching. For the Scripture says, "Do not muzzle the ox while it is treading out the grain," and "The worker deserves his wages." 1 Timothy 5:17–18.

We ask you, brothers, to respect those who work hard among you, who are over you in the Lord and who admonish you. Hold them in the highest regard in love because of their work. Live in peace with each other.
1 Thessalonians 5:12–13

Obey your leaders and submit to their authority. They keep watch over you as men who must give an account. Obey them so that their work will be a joy, not a burden, for that would be of no advantage to you. Hebrews 13:17

Lucas Cranach the Elder (1472–1553). *Wittenberg Altar Tryptych.*

Faith comes by hearing.[Tu] That's the essence of the church's life and mission. God sends forth His Holy Spirit by the preaching of His Word and the administration of His Sacraments. And the Spirit of God creates faith in Christ when and where He pleases in those who hear the Gospel.[W]

Lucas Cranach's painting clearly depicts the two holy orders at the heart of the church's life: preachers and hearers. The congregation listens in rapt attention at the sound of the preacher's words.[Th] The preacher does not preach about an absent Christ; He *preaches Christ*.[F] In the faithful preaching of His Gospel, Jesus Christ Himself creates and sustains faith by the power of His Holy Spirit. Note that Jesus' loincloth is blown in two directions at once, depicting the work of the Holy Spirit, who "blows wherever He wills" wherever the Gospel is proclaimed.

Pray for your pastor that He may preach God's Word faithfully.[S] And pray that God's Spirit may open the ears and hearts of all who hear, for their souls' salvation.

Meditations: Change Blessing Praise Request
[M]Read the article on page 115. [Tu]Romans 10:8–17. What is "*the* message"?
[W]1 Corinthians 12:1–6. How do you know you have God's Spirit? [Th]1 Corinthians 1:20–31. What can you boast about today?
[F]Galatians 2:15–3:1. How do Paul's words connect with this painting? [S]Ephesians 6:18–24. Offer prayers specifically for your pastor.

Remarkable symbolism fills Holbein's painting *The French Ambassadors*, identifying areas of government responsibility and interest, from fine arts to foreign affairs. But one detail teaches the Christian view of government: the open book on the lower table, which contains a hymn of the Ten Commandments.

The Lord's Arm of the Law

This open book reminds us that civil government is the strong arm of the law to maintain order in this world. From earliest recorded history, the authority of government has stood on God's commandments.[Tu]

However, this open book of the Ten Commandments also reminds us that civil government is the strong arm of the Lord Himself. The Lord instituted government to keep order in this world, an authority recognized also by Jesus.[W] Not only should we submit to government authority "for the Lord's sake,"[Th] we should also pray for those in authority over us. This pleases God our Savior and also speaks well of our Christian faith.[F]

The Lord's Arm of the Gospel

Alongside His Law and government, God also provided His Gospel and the church. Through the Gospel, the Lord takes away our offenses. He restores us as citizens of His kingdom.[S] Though the Law is God's strong arm to rule and condemn, the Gospel is His strong arm to save.

Hans Holbein the Younger (1497/98–1543). *The French Ambassadors.*

OF CIVIL GOVERNMENT

p36

Everyone must submit himself to the governing authorities, for there is no authority except that which God has established. The authorities that exist have been established by God. Consequently, he who rebels against the authority is rebelling against what God has instituted, and those who do so will bring judgment on themselves. For rulers hold no terror for those who do right, but for those who do wrong. Do you want to be free from fear of the one in authority? Then do what is right and he will commend you. For he is God's servant to do you good. But if you do wrong, be afraid, for he does not bear the sword for nothing. He is God's servant, an agent of wrath to bring punishment on the wrongdoer. Romans 13:1–4

OF CITIZENS

p37

Give to Caesar what is Caesar's, and to God what is God's. Matthew 22:21

It is necessary to submit to the authorities, not only because of possible punishment but also because of conscience. This is also why you pay taxes, for the authorities are God's servants, who give their full time to governing. Give everyone what you owe him: If you owe taxes, pay taxes; if revenue, then revenue; if respect, then respect; if honor, then honor. Romans 13:5–7

I urge, then, first of all, that requests, prayers, intercession and thanksgiving be made for everyone—for kings and all those in authority, that we may live peaceful and quiet lives in all godliness and holiness. This is good, and pleases God our Savior. 1 Timothy 2:1–3

Remind the people to be subject to rulers and authorities, to be obedient, to be ready to do whatever is good. Titus 3:1

Submit yourselves for the Lord's sake to every authority instituted among men: whether to the king, as the supreme authority, or to governors, who are sent by him to punish those who do wrong and to commend those who do right. 1 Peter 2:13–14

Meditations: Change Blessing Praise Request

M Read the article on page 116. Tu Deuteronomy 10:14–11:2. What did God's arm accomplish?
W Matthew 22:15–22. What belongs to God? Th 1 Peter 2:9–17. Why do good works in response to God's mercy?
F 1 Thessalonians 4. Reflect on your ambitions. S Ephesians 2:11–22. How did you gain access to the Father's kingdom?

Douglas MacArthur once commented, "The fathers plant the tree; the children live in its shade." In the *Circle of Love*, the "shade" of father and mother falls on their child to form a loving family circle.[Tu]

Circle Intact

How nicely the loving arms of both parents outline the circle of love in the lively colors and gentle lines of the picture. The child rests calmly and securely in parental shade. Truly blessed are those families in which the father is regularly present to provide his share of the shade from the heat of everyday life,[W] in which the mother adds faithful love and nurture,[Th] in which the children live in the shadow of a loving relationship between husband and wife. Such children enjoy a special shade throughout their lives that is likely to extend its benefits into future generations.

Circle Broken

How different is the picture when the family circle is fractured. How the shade dissipates when the arms of father and mother work at cross-purposes.[F] How much more difficult it can be for a single set of arms to fully complete the circle and to provide all of the nurturing shade that a child needs. How difficult for children to grow up in surroundings of fear and family secrets, in the absence of loving discipline. The absence of strong and loving arms can result in more heat than young minds and hearts can bear, a failure that too often ends up repeated in succeeding generations, mirrored in adult lives and passed along to others.

Circle Restored

How important that the family circle and its shade be restored for the children. This is always possible because of the shade that the Lord provides[S] under the cross of His Son, who enables new beginnings any and every time, including when the circle of love in a family becomes broken.

TO HUSBANDS

p38

Husbands, in the same way be considerate as you live with your wives, and treat them with respect as the weaker partner and as heirs with you of the gracious gift of life, so that nothing will hinder your prayers. 1 Peter 3:7

Husbands, love your wives and do not be harsh with them. Colossians 3:19

TO WIVES

p38

Wives, submit to your husbands as to the Lord. Ephesians 5:22

They were submissive to their own husbands, like Sarah, who obeyed Abraham and called him her master. You are her daughters if you do what is right and do not give way to fear. 1 Peter 3:5–6

TO PARENTS

p38

Fathers, do not exasperate your children; instead, bring them up in the training and instruction of the Lord. Ephesians 6:4

TO CHILDREN

p38

Children, obey your parents in the Lord, for this is right. "Honor your father and your mother"— which is the first commandment with a promise— "that it may go well with you and that you may enjoy long life on the earth." Ephesians 6:1–3

Michael Escoffery (contemporary). *Circle of Love.*

Meditations: Change Blessing Praise Request

^MRead the article on page 118.

^{Tu}Psalm 128. What blessings does this psalm describe? ^WProverbs 23:15–25. How does the heavenly Father model genuine fatherhood?

ThProverbs 31:10–31. What makes a woman praiseworthy? ^FGenesis 3:6–13. How do God's actions show His heart in this passage?

^SPsalm 121. Where does your help come from?

Greek → *doulos = servant (read Philemon)*
→ *in Greek, no difference between servant + slave*

P38-39

P 39

TO WORKERS OF ALL KINDS

Slaves, obey your earthly masters with respect and fear, and with sincerity of heart, just as you would obey Christ. Obey them not only to win their favor when their eye is on you, but like slaves of Christ, doing the will of God from your heart. Serve wholeheartedly, as if you were serving the Lord, not men, because you know that the Lord will reward everyone for whatever good he does, whether he is slave or free.
Ephesians 6:5–8

TO EMPLOYERS AND SUPERVISORS

Masters, treat your slaves in the same way. Do not threaten them, since you know that He who is both their Master and yours is in heaven, and there is no favoritism with Him.
Ephesians 6:9

Georges de la Tour (1593–1652). *St. Joseph, the Carpenter.*

Meditations: Change Blessing Praise Request
M Read the article on page 121. Tu Matthew 13:53–58. How do you regard Christ? W Luke 2:41–52. How did Christ regard His parents?
Th John 8:12–20. What do followers of Christ enjoy? F Matthew 5. What do others see in you?
S 1 Thessalonians 5:12–15. How is God's work described in this passage?

The French painter Georges de la Tour shows Jesus assisting His stepfather, Joseph. Notice Jesus' hand silhouetted against the candle, revealing not only the bones in His fingers but the dirt beneath His nails! Christ got His hands dirty in Joseph's shop.[Tu]

Humble Service

Jesus did what His stepfather asked Him to do: "Here, Son, hold the light so your father can see." Sound familiar? Did your father ever give you that menial task when you were a child? You carefully held the flashlight so your dad could see. This was crucial to avoid hearing that reprimand, "I said hold the light right here. And hold it still, please!" How humiliating!

Even though Jesus was the Maker of heaven and earth, He humbled Himself by submitting to His parents and the clients they served with their trade.[W] He did this to assist their service to others and honor His Father in heaven.

When Jesus served His earthly parents—His employers—He was also serving His Father in heaven. According to His human nature, Jesus lived like you and me. He humbled Himself not only in obedience to the cross, but also as a child in obedience to His parents.

Light of the Word

Appropriately, de la Tour's painting of Christ holding the light for Joseph also reminds us that Jesus was the Light for His stepfather, His mother, and for the whole world![Th] His humble service in the carpenter's shop foreshadowed His humble service on the cross. He became light for us so that we may never walk in darkness. He is the Light that shines and dispels the darkness of our sin.

Now, if Jesus asked you to do something like hold the light for Him in the carpenter's shop, you probably wouldn't give it a second thought. You would feel honored to assist the Savior of the world (even if the task seemed menial). Well, guess what? He asks you to do just that. He asks you to uphold your calling in life as a worker. Hold it steady no matter what your vocation is. Walk in faith to the Lord while eagerly glorifying God with your labor. This is the life work of every Christian, no matter your trade, skill, or occupation.[F]

When you serve faithfully at what you do, you glorify the Lord. From His love for you, you serve wholeheartedly. Through His perfect obedience to the Father, He gave His life on the cross to save you from your sins.[S]

A young woman gazes into a mirror. But what does she see? Perhaps she sees someone who believes such advertising slogans as "Indulge yourself," "You deserve a break," and "You're worth it," all of which invite her to make herself the center of her universe. Or perhaps she sees a person who believes she ought not care for herself at all. Maybe she is that sort of Christian who would live so selflessly that she would neglect her own needs and risk running herself down.

To balance these extreme views of yourself, the Scripture says, "Love your neighbor as yourself."[Tu]

Love Your Neighbor

The Scripture commands that you "honor one another above yourselves"[W] and share your faith with others so that they might also know God's forgiving love. By showing love for others—including enemies— in this way, you show love for your Lord. Your love for your neighbor expresses faith and trust in Jesus: "Whatever you did for one of the least of these brothers of Mine, you did for Me."[Th]

Love Yourself

But such love for your neighbor does not mean that you must abuse yourself and neglect your own needs! Rather, follow your Lord's example, both praying for yourself (something many Christians hesitate to do) and caring for yourself, in order that you might be strengthened to serve.[F]

A Christian's self-care goes much deeper than prayer and rest. You care for yourself by looking into God's Word, which strengthens your faith and gives you love for your neighbor. You care for yourself by daily returning to your Baptism. You care for yourself through regular participation in Holy Communion. The Lord provides these precious means to sustain you and prepare you as a witness for His kingdom.

Look into the mirror of your own life, Christian! See there not the center of your own universe, but rather the center of God's universe—that He loved you so much that He gave His Son to die for you.[S]

TO YOUTH

p39

Young men, in the same way be submissive to those who are older. All of you, clothe yourselves with humility toward one another, because, "God opposes the proud but gives grace to the humble." Humble yourselves, therefore, under God's mighty hand, that He may lift you up in due time. 1 Peter 5:5–6

TO WIDOWS

p39

The widow who is really in need and left all alone puts her hope in God and continues night and day to pray and to ask God for help. But the widow who lives for pleasure is dead even while she lives. 1 Timothy 5:5–6

TO EVERYONE

p39

The commandments . . . are summed up in this one rule: "Love your neighbor as yourself." Romans 13:9

I urge . . . that requests, prayers, intercession and thanksgiving be made for everyone. 1 Timothy 2:1

James Abbott McNeill Whistler (1834–1903). *The Little White Girl: Symphony in White No. 2.*

Meditations: Change Blessing Praise Request

M Read the article on page 122. Tu Leviticus 19:9–18. What sentence repeats throughout this passage? Why?
W Romans 12:1–10. What is the basis of worship? Th Matthew 25:31–46. What has Christ prepared for you?
F Luke 22:39–44. What reason does Jesus give for praying for yourself? S John 17:6–19. Whom does Jesus pray for and why?

CHRISTIAN QUESTIONS WITH THEIR ANSWERS

After confession and instruction in the Ten Commandments, the Creed, the Lord's Prayer, and the Sacraments of Baptism and the Lord's Supper, the pastor may ask, or Christians may ask themselves these questions:

1. *Do you believe that you are a sinner?*

> Yes, I believe it. I am a sinner.

2. *How do you know this?*

> From the Ten Commandments, which I have not kept.

3. *Are you sorry for your sins?*

> Yes, I am sorry that I have sinned against God.

4. *What have you deserved from God because of your sins?*

> His wrath and displeasure, temporal death, and eternal damnation.
> See Romans 6:21, 23.

5. *Do you hope to be saved?*

> Yes, that is my hope.

6. *In whom then do you trust?*

> In my dear Lord Jesus Christ.

7. *Who is Christ?*

> The Son of God, true God and man.

8. *How many Gods are there?*

> Only one, but there are three persons: Father, Son, and Holy Spirit.

9. *What has Christ done for you that you trust in Him?*

> He died for me and shed His blood for me on the cross for the forgiveness of sins.

10. *Did the Father also die for you?*

> He did not. The Father is God only, as is the Holy Spirit; but the Son is both true God and true man. He died for me and shed His blood for me.

11. *How do you know this?*

> From the holy Gospel, from the words instituting the Sacrament, and by His body and blood given me as a pledge in the Sacrament.

12. *What are the words of institution?*

> Our Lord Jesus Christ, on the night when He was betrayed, took bread, and when He had given thanks, He broke it and gave it to the disciples and said: "Take, eat; this is My body, which is given for you. This do in remembrance of Me."

124

In the same way also He took the cup after supper, and when He had given thanks, He gave it to them, saying: "Drink of it, all of you; this cup is the new testament in My blood, which is shed for you for the forgiveness of sins. This do, as often as you drink it, in remembrance of Me."

13. *Do you believe, then, that the true body and blood of Christ are in the Sacrament?*

Yes, I believe it.

14. *What convinces you to believe this?*

The word of Christ: Take, eat, this is My body; drink of it, all of you, this is My blood.

15. *What should we do when we eat His body and drink His blood, and in this way receive His pledge?*

We should remember and proclaim His death and the shedding of His blood, as He taught us: This do, as often as you drink it, in remembrance of Me.

16. *Why should we remember and proclaim His death?*

First, so that we may learn to believe that no creature could make satisfaction for our sins. Only Christ, true God and man, could do that. Second, so we may learn to be horrified by our sins, and to regard them as very serious. Third, so we may find joy and comfort in Christ alone, and through faith in Him be saved.

17. *What motivated Christ to die and make full payment for your sins?*

His great love for His Father and for me and other sinners, as it is written in John 14; Romans 5; Galatians 2; and Ephesians 5.

18. *Finally, why do you wish to go to the Sacrament?*

That I may learn to believe that Christ, out of great love, died for my sin, and also learn from Him to love God and my neighbor.

19. *What should admonish and encourage a Christian to receive the Sacrament frequently?*

First, both the command and the promise of Christ the Lord. Second, his own pressing need, because of which the command, encouragement, and promise are given.

20. *But what should you do if you are not aware of this need and have no hunger and thirst for the Sacrament?*

To such a person no better advice can be given than this: first, he should touch his body to see if he still has flesh and blood. Then he should believe what the Scriptures say of it in Galatians 5 and Romans 7.

Second, he should look around to see whether he is still in the world, and remember that there will be no lack of sin and trouble, as the Scriptures say in John 15–16 and in 1 John 2 and 5.

Third, he will certainly have the devil also around him, who with his lying and murdering day and night will let him have no peace, within or without, as the Scriptures picture him in John 8 and 16; 1 Peter 5; Ephesians 6; and 2 Timothy 2.

Art Credits

2. Gaudenzio Ferrari (1475–1546; Italian Renaissance). *Musical Angels*. Sanctuary, Saronno, Italy. © Scala/Art Resource, NY.
10. Marie Spartali Stillman (1844–1927; Pre-Raphaelite). *Beatrice*. Delaware Art Museum, Wilmington, DE, USA/Samuel and Mary R. Bancroft Memorial/Visual Arts Library, London, UK. Bridgeman Art Library.
12. Fra Angelico (1387–1455; Italian Gothic). *The Conversion of St. Augustine*. Musee Thomas Henry, Cherbourg, France. © Giraudon/Art Resource, NY.

The Ten Commandments

16. Karl Pavlovitch Briullov (1799–1852; Russian Romanticism). *The Last Days of Pompeii* (1833). Russian State Museum, St. Petersburg, Russia. © Scala/Art Resource, NY.
19. Nicolas Poussin (1594–1665; French Baroque/Classicism). *Christ Healing the Blind at Jericho*. Louvre, Paris, France. © Réunion des Musées Nationaux/Art Resource, NY.
20. Pieter Brueghel the Elder (1525/30–1569; Dutch Northern Renaissance). *Fight between Carnival and Lent* (1559). Kunsthistorishes Museum, Vienna, Austria. © Erich Lessing/Art Resource, NY.
23. Gustav Adolph Spangenberg (1828–1891; German Romanticism). *Luther in His Family Circle* (1866). Museum der bildenden Künte, Leipzig. Bridgeman Art Library.
24. Chinese School (19th century). *Eugene Pottier Writing 'The International'*. Private collection. Bridgeman Art Library.
27. François Boucher (1703–1770, French Rococo). *Lovers in the Park*. Agnew and Sons, London, UK. Bridgeman Art Library.
28. Rafael Tejeo (1798–1856; Spanish Neoclassicism). *The Good Samaritan*. Caylus Anticuario, Madrid. Bridgeman Art Library.
31. Paul Gauguin (1848–1903; French Post-Impressionism). *Ta Matete* (1892). Kunstmuseum, Basel, Switzerland. © Giraudon/Art Resource, NY.
32. Hieronymus Bosch (Dutch Northern Renaissance). *The Haywain: central panel of the triptych* (c. 1500). Monasterio de El Escorial, Spain. Bridgeman Art Library.
35. Limbourgh Brothers (15th century; Franco/Flemish Late Gothic). *October, Tres Riches Heures* (1416). Musee Conde, Chantilly, France. © Réunion des Musée Nationaux/Art Resource, NY.
36. Taddeo Gaddi (c.1300–1366; Italian Late Gothic). *Tree of Life (Tree of the Cross)*. Museo dell'Opera, S. Croce, Florence, Italy. © Scala/Art Resource, NY.

The Apostles' Creed

41. Titian (c.1488–1576; Italian Late Renaissance). *Adoration of the Trinity*. Museo del Prado, Madrid, Spain. © Scala/Art Resource, NY.
42. Honoré Daumier (1808–1879; French Realism). *The Kiss, or A Man and His Child*. Musee d'Orsay, Paris, France. © Erich Lessing/Art Resource, NY.
45. Master Bertram of Minden (c.1345–c.1415; German Gothic). Inner left wing of the high altar of St. Peter's in Hamburg, *The Grabower Altar*. Hamburg Kunsthalle, Hamburg, Germany. Bridgeman Art Library.
46. Fra Angelico (1387–1455; Italian Gothic). *Annunciation*. Museo del Prado, Madrid, Spain. © Scala/Art Resource, NY.
49. Hans Holbein the Younger (1497/98–1543; German Northern Renaissance). *Allegory of the Old and New Testaments*. National Gallery of Scotland, Edinburgh, Scotland. Bridgeman Art Library.
50. Gustave Doré (1832–1883; French Romantic/Realism). *Christ Leaving the Praetorian*. Musee des Beaux-Arts, Nantes, France. © Giraudon/Art Resource, NY.
53. Jean François Millet (1814–1875; French Realism). *La Petite Bergere*. Louvre, Paris, France. © Giraudon/Art Resource, NY.
54. Titian (c.1488–1576; Italian Late Renaissance). *Pentecost*. S. Maria della Salute, Venice, Italy. © Scala/Art Resource, NY.
57. John Vanderlyn (1775–1852; American Neoclassicism). *The Landing of Columbus*. U.S. Capitol Building Rotunda. Architect of the Capitol.
58. Victor-Louis Mottez (1809–1897; French Romanticism). *The Resurrection of the Dead*. Musee des Beaux-Arts, Lille, France. © Giraudon/Art Resource, N.Y.
61. Gaudenzio Ferrari (1475–1546; Italian Renaissance). *Musical Angels*. Sanctuary, Saronno, Italy. © Scala/Art Resource, NY.

The Lord's Prayer

64. Michelangelo (1475–1564; Italian Renaissance). *The Creation of Adam*. Sistine Chapel, Vatican Palace, Vatican State. © Scala/Art Resource, NY.

67. Raphael (1483–1520; Italian Renaissance). *Moses and the Burning Bush*. Logee, Vatican Palace, Vatican State. © Scala/Art Resource, NY.

68. Peter Paul Rubens (1577–1640; Flemish Baroque). *The Defeat of Sannacherib, King of Assur*. Alte Pinakothek, Munich, Germany. © Erich Lessing/Art Resource, NY.

71. Thomas Hart Benton (1889–1975; American Regionalism). *Prayer* (American Historical Epic, c.1919–1924). The Nelson-Atkins Museum of Art, Kansas City, Missouri (Bequest of the artist) F75-21/4.

72. Jean François Millet (1814–1875; French Realism). *The Angelus* (1857). Musee d'Orsay, Paris, France. © Erich Lessing/Art Resource, NY.

75. Lucas Cranach the Elder (1472–1553; German Northern Renaissance). *Christ and the Woman Taken in Adultery*. Museo e Gallerie Nazionali di Capodimonte, Naples, Italy. Bridgeman Art Library.

76. Piero di Cosimo (1462–1521; Italian Renaissance). *Simonetta Vespucci*. Musee Conde, Chantilly, France. © Giraudon/Art Resource, NY.

79. Francesco de Rosa, called Pacecco (1607–1656; Italian Baroque). *The Martyrdom of St. Lawrence*.

80. Giovanni Francesco Guercino (1591–1666; Italian Baroque). *The Incredulity of St. Thomas*. Pinacoteca, Vatican Museums, Vatican State. © Scala/Art Resource, NY.

The Means of Grace

85. Emma Brownlow (1832–1905; English Romanticism). *The Christening* (1863). Coram Foundation, London. Bridgeman Art Library.

86. Lucas Cranach the Elder (1472–1553; German Northern Renaissance). *Wittenberg Altar Tryptych*. Church of St. Marien, Wittenberg, Germany. Bridgeman Art Library.

89. John Gadsby Chapman (1808–1889; American Romanticism). *Baptism of Pocahontas* (1840). U.S. Capitol Building Rotunda. Architect of the Capitol.

90. Hippolyte-Paul Delaroche (1797–1856; French Neoclassicism/Romanticism). *The Young Martyr*. Louvre, Paris, France. Peter Willi/Bridgeman Art Library.

93. Lorenzo Lotto (Italian, Venetian, born about 1480, died 1556). *Brother Gregoro Belo of Vicenza*, 1547. (Oil on canvas, 34⅜ × 28 in.; 87.3 × 71.1 cm) The Metropolitan Museum of Art, Rogers Fund, 1965. (65.117) Photograph © 1996 The Metropolitan Museum of Art.

94. Georges de la Tour (1593–1652; French Baroque). *The Penitent Magdalen*. The Metropolitan Museum of Art, Gift of Mr. and Mrs. Charles Wrightsman, 1978. (1978.517) Photograph © 1997 The Metropolitan Museum of Art.

97. Nicolas Poussin (1594–1665; French Baroque/Classicism). *The Sacrament of Ordination* (1647). Duke of Sutherland Collection/National Gallery of Scotland. Bridgeman Art Library.

98. Florentine School (Italian Renaissance). *Antonio Hurling Dung* (1502). Museo Stibbert, Florence, Italy. © Nicolo Orsi Battaglini/Art Resource, NY.

101. Northern Renaissance. *Altar Frontal from Torslunde Church* (1561). Photo: Niels Elswing. National Museum, Copenhagen, Denmark.

102. Salvador Dali (1904–1989; Spanish Surrealism). *The Last Supper* (1955). National Gallery of Art, Washington, D.C. Bridgeman Art Library.

105. Carl Friedrich Lessing (1808–1880; German Romanticism). *Hussite Sermon*. Staatliche Museen zu Berlin— Preussischer Kulturbesitz Nationalgalerie. Consignment 1836. Photo: Walter Klein, Düsseldorf 1998.

106. SIQUEIROS, David Alfaro. *The Sob*. 1939. Enamel on composition board, 48½″ × 24¾″ (123.2 × 62.9 cm). The Museum of Modern Art, New York. Given anonymously. Photograph © 2001 The Museum of Modern Art, New York.

Daily Devotion

111. Henry Le Jeune (1819–1904; English Romanticism). *A Prayer*. Private collection. © Art Resource, NY.

112. Henry Ossawa Tanner (1859–1937; American Realism). *The Thankful Poor*. Private collection. © Art Resource, NY.

115. Lucas Cranach the Elder (1472–1553; German Northern Renaissance). *Wittenberg Altar Tryptych*. Church of St. Marien, Wittenberg, Germany. Bridgeman Art Library.

116. Hans Holbein the Younger (1497/98–1543; German Northern Renaissance). *The French Ambassadors* (1533). National Gallery, London, Great Britain. © Erich Lessing/Art Resource, NY.

119. Michael Escoffery (contemporary; Jamaican American). *Circle of Love* (1996). Private collection. © Michael Escoffery/Art Resource, NY.

120. Georges de la Tour (1593–1652; French Baroque). *St. Joseph, the Carpenter*. Louvre, Paris, France. © Giraudon/Art Resource, NY.

123. James Abbott McNeill Whistler (1834–1903; American Aestheticism). *The Little White Girl: Symphony in White No. 2* (1864). © Tate Gallery, London/Art Resource, NY.

An Outline of Artistic Periods